Something Good

Available at:
www.amazon.com/author/larryoneal
(use lowercase letters)

DEDICATION

This book is dedicated to God through whom all things are possible. If it were not for Him, I could do nothing. He is the lifter of my head and the very breath I breathe. He is the reason for each of my heartbeats.

I also dedicate this book to my family and to you the reader. It is with great hope that someone will listen to these words God has given to me, for a time such as these. Always allow God to guide you on your journey through this life and into the next.

In Loving Memory of our Grandson
We will Love You forever son.

Dustin Haberle,
Mar. 4, 1995 – May 31, 2020
Pasco County, Firefighter EMT #2367

A man who loved God, had a heart of gold, and
served his community.

His moto was,
"Love More, Hate Less"

Table of Contents

Forward

In this book and others, I include God's word in my writings along with true life examples. Perhaps some of the examples are humorous but all are absolutely true and intended to give God all of the glory. It is only by His love and grace that I am here to share with my family and you my friends.

This book is titled; "Tell Me Something Good". So I will tell you the best news ever told. God loves you so much that He gave His only Begotten Son that you may have eternal life.

John 3:16 "For God so loved the world, that he gave his only begotten Son, that whosoever believeth in him should not perish, but have everlasting life."

If that was the end of the story, it should be more than enough for a glorious eternal life. It would be a life so wonderful that human words cannot begin to describe it. But I will tell you of other spectacular things yet to come.

Jesus said in **John 14:1-3** *"Let not your heart be troubled: ye believe in God, believe also in me. In my Father's house are many mansions: if it were not so, I would have told you. I go to prepare a place for you. And if I go and prepare a place for you, I will come again, and receive you unto myself; that where I am,* there *ye may be also."*

Since Jesus left Earth, He has been preparing a place for you more spectacular and wonderful than human words can describe. But best of all, we will remain with Jesus throughout all of eternity. One day He will most certainly return to take us with Him to our Heavenly home.

He is a God full of love and grace. He has given His very best that you might be saved and spend eternity with Him. Will you give Him any less than you're very best in return? Hopefully, you have already or will very soon choose Him and have many blessings. If you do not choose Him, you will have the exact opposite of blessings. He has left the choice up to you.

The choice that He has left up to you is, will you serve and live your life for Him and accept His gift of salvation? If you do, you will have a much happier life here and in the life that is sure to come. But the choice is totally up to you. It is your decision and no one can make it for you. Which way will you choose?

Joshua 24:15 "And if it seem evil unto you to serve the LORD, choose you this day whom ye will serve; whether the gods which your fathers served that were on the other side of the flood, or the gods of the Amorites, in whose land ye dwell: but as for me and my house, we will serve the LORD."

John 14:6 "Jesus said unto him, I am the way, the truth, and the life: no man cometh unto the Father, but by me."

John 14:16 is the reason that we pray to Jesus. He alone is able to save us and no one else. He alone is to be our Savior. He alone is the ultimate sacrifice for our sins. It is through His shed blood that we are saved. He is the door through which we have access to our Heavenly Father. Without going through the door, we cannot hope to communicate with or reach our Heavenly Father.

John 9:31 "Now we know that God heareth not sinners: but if any man be a worshipper of God, and doeth his will, him he heareth."

John 14:6" Jesus said unto him, I am the way, the truth, and the life: no man cometh unto the Father, but by me."

From Adam and Eve sinning in the Garden of Eden to the crucifixion of Jesus Christ, sins were cleansed by animal sacrifice. Each animal sacrificed had to be without spot or blemish. Jesus Christ was without spot or blemish and without sin. He had God's DNA throughout His body and was perfect in every way. He became the Holy sacrifice for our sins. Without His selfless, sacrifice we would be eternally lost to sin. We owe Him more than we could ever repay.

He Is

1 John 4:16 "And we have known and believed the love that God hath to us. God is love; and he that dwells in love dwells in God, and God in him."

Yes, God is love but remember that good and evil cannot reside in the same place at the same time. You cannot have light and darkness in the same place at the same time. With both of these, you will have one or the other. You must choose which you will have as it is your choice. Please choose wisely because it will affect your life now and the life which is sure to come.

Psalms 103:1 "Bless the LORD, O my soul: and all that is within me, bless His holy name."

Psalms 103:2 "Bless the LORD, O my soul, and forget not all His benefits:"

Psalms 103:3 "Who forgives all thine iniquities; who heals all your diseases;"

Psalms 103:4 "Who redeems your life from destruction; who crowns thee with loving kindness and tender mercies;"

Psalms 103:5 "Who satisfies your mouth with good things; so that your youth is renewed like the eagle's."

Psalms 103:6 "The LORD executes righteousness and judgment for all that are oppressed."

Psalms 103:7 "He made known his ways unto Moses, his acts unto the children of Israel."

Psalms 103:8 "The LORD is merciful and gracious, slow to anger, and plenteous in mercy."

Psalms 103:9 "He will not always strive with us: nor will he keep his anger forever."

Psalms 103:10 "He hath not dealt with us after our sins; nor rewarded us according to our iniquities."

Psalms 103:11 "For as the heaven is high above the earth, so great is his mercy toward them that fear him."

Psalms 103:12 "As far as the east is from the west, so far hath he removed our transgressions from us."

Psalms 103:13 "Like as a father feels sympathy for his children, so the LORD feels sympathy for them that fear him."

Psalms 103:14 "For he knows our frame; he remembers that we are dust."

Psalms 103:15 "As for man, his days are as grass: as a flower of the field, so he flourishes."

Psalms 103:16 "For the wind passes over it, and it is gone; and the place thereof shall know it no more."

Psalms 103:17 " *But the mercy of the LORD is from everlasting to everlasting upon them that fear him, and his righteousness unto children's children;"*

Psalms 103:18 *"To such as keep his covenant, and to those that remember his commandments to do them."*

Psalms 103:19 *"The LORD hath prepared his throne in the heavens; and his kingdom rules over all."*

Psalms 103:20 *"Bless the LORD, ye his angels, that excel in strength, that do his commandments, hearkening unto the voice of his word."*

Psalms 103:21 *"Bless ye the LORD, all ye his hosts; ye ministers of his, that do his pleasure.'*

Psalms 103:22 *"Bless the LORD, all his works in all places of his dominion: bless the LORD, O my soul."*

God loves you intently but requires our love and obedience. He knows what will destroy us in the end and He doesn't want that to happen to us. It is my desire for you my family, and friends that we listen to Him as intently as He loves us.

He knows we will stumble but that is the time for us to repent. Ask for His forgiveness and do our very best not to do it again.

1 John 1:9 *"If we confess our sins, he is faithful and just to forgive us our sins, and to cleanse us from all unrighteousness".*

The Morning

Matthew 10:22 "And ye shall be hated of all men for my name's sake: but he that endure to the end shall be saved."

As I sit here in the wee hours of the morning, I ask myself what I am doing up hours before dawn? I woke up shortly after three o'clock in the morning and let three dogs out in the backyard for a few minutes. There is a Jack Russel named Luke, a Poodle named Tosha, and a Yorkie named Sophie. Although very small, Sophie is the ring leader and hunter of the three. Luke is our son Larry Brentt's dog, who is visiting with us.

Task completed, I returned to bed. It is after only a few moments that the Lord says, "I have some writing for you to do." So here I sit writing what the Lord instructs me to write. It is for His witness that I share with you the things of my life. It is with these true events that you may see a few of the wonders of God and His love for us, His blessings and protection.

~ 14 ~

According to the Holy Bible, God came down and walked with Adam and Eve in the cool of the day. Have you ever wondered what time "the cool of the day" is? Have you ever awaken around 3 o'clock in the morning with things of God on your mind? Most people that I have asked this reply that they awake about that time of the morning when God wants to talk to them. God speaks to us at all times of the day and night, but around three o'clock in the morning seems to work best.

This time of day is quiet with plenty of room to listen. The hustle and bustle of our day, has not begun as of yet. Our minds give extra thought to many things during this part of the day. It is also a chance to start a new day afresh having faith for better things than the day before. This is when God talks to me the most. When does God speak to you with that soft, loving, voice?

You can tell it is God speaking to you when He speaks love and encouragement. Sometimes He is speaking instructions of something that He wants you to do. Occasionally He speaks correction to you. Sometimes he speaks of hope and faith but He always speaks with love.

Job 33:15 *"In a dream, in a vision of the night, when deep sleep falls upon men, in slumbering upon the bed;"*

Job 33:16 *"Then he opens the ears of men, and seals their instruction."*

Sometimes you will have someone on your mind very strong. You may not know what that person is in need of, but stop and pray for them immediately. You may have averted a disaster in that person's life at that very moment by praying for them. Later on, you may find out the reason that you prayed for them. But whether you find out or not, you have done what God wanted. When you hear God speaking to you, it is time to listen very closely. Follow the listening by doing what God instructs you to do. Always be obedient to God!

Before beginning to write the first book, everything seemed to be going normal. As I began to write, things began changing. At first, it began with simple distractions. It seemed as though every time I sat down to write, the phone would ring. If it wasn't that, it was something else. It wasn't anything Earth shattering, but it was just simple things in the beginning.

The more I wrote the more intense things became. The distractions grew until they were impossible to ignore any longer. It became so apparent that even a blind man could see what was happening. Someone or something did not want me to write and was hindering my efforts.

To counteract the distractions, each time I sit down to write, I would say a simple prayer. I prayed, "Heavenly Father give me the things you want me to write in this book. Tell me exactly how you want me to put those things in this book for your glory. All of you Father and none of me is my prayer, in Jesus' Holy name I pray, Amen".

After writing about forty pages for this book, I began having a sinus issue. I have had sinus issues in the past as flowers and trees begin to bloom. But I have not had any sinus issues in the last five years. It always begins with congested sinus', followed by a slight cough and a scratchy throat. I usually self-medicate for a few days but then wind up at the doctor's office.

Last week my sinuses became stuffy. I had a slight cough, followed by a scratchy throat. I was way more tired than usual but attributed the tiredness to some of the over the counter medications. I prayed that God would touch me and heal me. I self-medicated and became much better after a few days.

I decided to call the doctor's office anyway. They told me that I would have to be tested for the Covid Virus and then go to an urgent care office as my doctor was out. They told me that they would call me back to confirm the Covid Virus test time. They never called me back, so I decided the test was no longer necessary.

Two days later they call me to schedule the Covid-19 test. I thought, "I don't need them now" and I started to tell them, "no thanks". Then I thought that perhaps I should go, get a prescription for antibiotics as spare medication for home.

I arrived in the doctor's parking lot and a nice lady came out and performed the test. She said,

"Sit tight and we will call you in twenty minutes with the results".

Twenty minutes passed and my phone rang. The nurse on the other end said, "You tested positive for Covid-19". I said, "You have got to be kidding"! Feeling as great as I did, I was shocked. I am now self-isolating and taking antibiotics along with over the counter medications.

I still feel great, praise God. When God has a plan, Satan has no choice but to get out of the way and let God have His way. If my wife and I had not begun praying when we did, there is no telling how much worse it would have gotten.

John 10:10 "The thief cometh not, but for to steal, and to kill, and to destroy: I am come that they might have life, and that they might have it more abundantly."

God has intervened many times in my life. It began with playing on poison ivy as a kid with no itching or anything else associated with that plant.

My sisters contracted various childhood sicknesses like measles when we were young. I would go in to play checkers or some other game with them. To this day I have not contracted any of the diseases associated with childhood. God has protected me all of my life for which I am extremely grateful. To God be the glory for His love, grace, mercy, protection and healing power.

Psalms 103:2 " Bless the LORD, O my soul, and forget not all His benefits:"

Psalms 103:3 "Who forgive all thine iniquities; who heals all your diseases;"

Psalms 103:4 "Who redeem your life from destruction; who crown thee with loving kindness and tender mercies;"

Psalms 103:5 "Who satisfies your mouth with good things; so that your youth is renewed like the eagle's."

God is a protector! He has protected me and He will protect you. But do not intentionally (on purpose) place yourself in a situation where you will need God's help. Do all that you can to stay safe and God will do the rest.

Placing yourself in a bad situation may result in God saying, "You got yourself into this situation, now deal with the consequences". If that is what He says, you can be sure of one thing, He will never leave or forsake you. He will go through the battle with you. It has now become a hard life lesson but with Him beside you and giving you strength, you will make it out the other side. Just keep your faith and eyes upon God and never doubt that He loves you. Only He can give you strength for all things.

Matthew 4:7 "Jesus said unto him, It is written again, You shalt not tempt the Lord your God."

Matthew 23:9 "And call no man your father upon the earth: for one is your Father, which is in heaven."

Until 2016, I worked for a major electrical company that generated electricity. Working in a coal fired power plant is noisy, very dirty, and very dangerous. The work was hard as a Journeyman Certified Welder and often in very strange places and positions.

After eleven years of power plant work, I sustained a back injury. Over the next couple of years, my back was injured two more times.

This back injury affected all phases of my life and made it almost unbearable. Most of the time I wore an electrical device to lessened the pain. It did not eliminate the pain but only lessened it to the point that I could just barely function. I could not perform normal activities with my family which also caused me anguish. With a young son and two daughters who needed my assistance and support, it was very difficult.

One night an evangelist came to our church and delivered the message. Towards the end of that service, prayer was offered for those who needed something from God.

I went forward for prayer for my back. The evangelist prayed for me and God touched my back that very night. Since that prayer, I have been able to go about my normal activities doing whatever it is that I need to do. I am still mindful of my back and I try not to push it too hard. I do not need to wear the electrical pain device any longer and have no back pain.

I try to listen to my body at all times. On one occasion, my son was told by a young man in his early twenties that I was a Bull. That simply means that I work hard and strong. I was in my sixties at that time and I give God the praise for that. That was praise to God as to His healing power and an encouraging word to me and my son. I am 71 years of age at the writing of this and praise God I have not slowed down at all. I did have to give up climbing trees as I realized, should I fall, I may not bounce as well as I use to. That was a joke.

Exodus 15:26 "And said, If thou wilt diligently hearken to the voice of the LORD thy God, and wilt do that which is right in his sight, and wilt give ear to his commandments, and keep all his statutes, I will put none of these diseases upon thee, which I have brought upon the Egyptians: for I am the LORD that healeth thee."

Psalms 103:3   *"Who forgives all thine iniquities; who heals all of your diseases;"*

In The Beginning

Genesis 1:1 "In the beginning God created the heaven and the Earth."

As the Bible begins, God created the heavens and the Earth. He created light and every living thing.

God created a beautiful garden and named it Eden. He created the first man and named him Adam. God instructed Adam to tend the garden and God created a helpmate for him named Eve.

Until this time Adam and Eve were totally innocent. They had no knowledge of good and evil, right or wrong. They only knew that they were and that God provided for them and loved them.

In the Bible, we read that God came down and walked and talked with Adam and Eve in the cool of the day. This demonstrated that God loved them and wanted to spend time with them. God must have enjoyed their company. He also gave them instructions.

Genesis 3:8 "And they heard the voice of the LORD God walking in the garden in the cool of the day: and Adam and his wife hid themselves from the presence of the LORD God amongst the trees of the garden."

When God created Adam and Eve, He gave them the ability to choose. This is called a "free will". A free will to make decisions for themselves but he hoped they would choose to listen to Him. He hoped that they would choose to love Him as much as He loved them.

If you love someone or something, you could prevent them from ever leaving you. You could chain them up or put them in a cage to prevent them from leaving. But if you did, how will you ever know if they truly love you? You must give them the choice, a "free will" to make their own decision. You must give them the choice to love you or not to love you.

We show God that we love Him by listening to Him through His Holy Word the Holy Bible and when He speaks to us. He only wants what is best for us. There are things and consequences out there that we do not know about even as older adults. There is an old saying that "talk is cheap and actions speak louder than words". What have you been showing God through your choices and actions?

John 14:15 "If you love me, keep my commandments."

You could go through life placing the blame on others, but what would that help? We would still be in the same situation that we currently are. We need to look closer at our own choices and compare them to the outcomes. Then we need to ask ourselves, "What could I have done differently to change that outcome for the better"?

It is not always the other person's actions that caused our resulting situations. Often it is our choices and things that we did not recognize that caused our problem.

God gave Adam and Eve one rule. God told Adam and Eve not to eat the fruit from the tree of "Knowledge of Good and Evil." God gave them only one rule which they did not obey.

In **Genesis 3:1-8,** the Bible tells us that in the garden, there was a serpent and the serpent was very subtle and persuasive. He gently persuaded Eve to try the fruit. Just a little seed of doubt, one little thought was all it started with and that was enough.

Genesis 3:6 "And when the woman saw that the tree was good for food, and that it was pleasant to the eyes, and a tree to be desired to make one wise, she took of the fruit thereof, and did eat, and gave also unto her husband with her; and he did eat."

The forbidden fruit must have tasted different than anything Eve had eaten before. The fruit must have tasted rather pleasant. So she did eat and then offered it to Adam and Adam did eat.

Genesis 3:3-4 "But of the fruit of the tree which is in the midst of the garden, God hath said, You shall not eat of it, neither shall ye touch it, lest ye die. And the serpent said unto the woman, You shall not surely die:"

What God had spoken of was spiritual death. What the serpent was speaking of was physical death. The two are very different types of death. The physical death has to do with the body dying. The spiritual death is not only the death of your soul but also the separation of man from God. Spiritual death is much worse than physical death. The body can only die once, but there can also be spiritual death.

Revelation 21:8 *"But the fearful, and unbelieving, and the abominable, and murderers, and whoremongers, and sorcerers, and idolaters, and all liars, shall have their part in the lake which burns with fire and brimstone: which is the second death."*

Sin usually begins with one single small thought. It is not a sin to have that one single thought. Satan will put thoughts of sin into your mind that should not be there. This is called temptation. It is a sin if we dwell upon a sinful thought or act upon it. The longer we think upon a sinful thought, the stronger it grows. Then it becomes something that we find is difficult to control. The next thing we know, we are caught in that sin trap.

At the first thought of sin, we should cast it down. We cast sin down by realizing it is not from God. We ask God to help remove that thought from our minds and then we start praising Jesus. Our enemy Satan, cannot stand it when we praise Jesus Christ. The more we praise Him the sooner Satan will leave you alone.

Bad dreams, sinful thoughts, feelings of depression, feelings of pending disaster and all things such as these are placed in your mind by Satan. The best way to remove them is not with medication. The best way to remove them is by praying them out. Start by rebuking Satan, binding him and those like him, and casting them out in the Holy Name of Jesus Christ.

You rebuke by realizing they are from Satan and you tell him so. Jesus Himself was tempted and had to rebuke Satan.

Luke 4:8 "And Jesus answered and said unto him, Get thee behind me, Satan:

for it is written, Thou shalt worship the Lord thy God, and him only shalt thou serve."

We as humans do not have the power within ourselves to do this. But through the power of Jesus Christ living in us and as saved children of God we certainly do. It is only through His power that we can hold at bay or cast out evil spirits.

Matthew 18:18 "Verily I say unto you, Whatsoever you shall bind on earth shall be bound in heaven: and whatsoever you shall loose on earth shall be loosed in heaven."

We then verbally bind that evil spirit in the Holy Name of Jesus Christ. Next, we start praising Jesus for delivering us. It won't be long before Satan just can't stand it any longer and has no choice but to leave you alone. Don't forget to keep believing that God will do what He has promised. Read your Bible so that you will know what His promises are for you. Keep your faith in Him no matter what you see or hear. Continued faith in

Him is the key to a child of God receiving their miracle and keeping it. Without continued faith, you may very well receive your miracle only to lose it if you doubt for a single moment.

As Adam and Eve ate the fruit, their eyes were opened spiritually and now they could see the difference between good and evil. After eating the forbidden fruit, they realized they were wearing no clothes and were ashamed. Realizing that they were naked, they ran and hid themselves from God. Now, they had a spiritual separation from God which is never a good thing. This was the fall of mankind and the spiritual death God spoke of.

The Bible tells us that God killed two animals and took their skins from which He made clothes for Adam and Eve. The shedding of blood to cover sin began here. Thus the price for sin is death as God killed the two animals to cover the sin of Adam and Eve.

Romans 6:23 *"For the wages of sin is death; but the gift of God is eternal life through Jesus Christ our Lord. "*

This established the guideline in the Old Testament; if a person committed a sin they were either stoned to death or redeemed (saved) by a blood sacrifice. The animal to be sacrificed was usually either, a lamb, doves, heifers (cows), or goats depending upon the sin a person committed. The sacrificed animal had to be without spot or blemish and the firstborn. Jesus Christ was the firstborn of God (only **begotten** son) and was without spot or blemish.

After reading this in the Bible, we do not read where God came down to walk and talk with Adam and Eve again.

During that time, people knew without a shadow of a doubt that God was real. God had demonstrated all too often for them to wonder if it was all true. God took a more direct approach to the elimination of sin and proving His power in the Old Testament. He sometimes caused the ground to open and swallow disobedient people.

Numbers 16:32 "And the earth opened her mouth, and swallowed them up, and their houses, and all the men that apper-tained *unto Korah, and all* their *goods."*

There was an occasion where He caused fire and brimstone to fall from the sky and destroyed two cities of sin and all who lived there.

Genesis 19:24 "Then the LORD rained upon Sodom and upon Gomorrah brim-stone and fire from the LORD out of heaven."

Genesis 19:25 "And he overthrew those cities, and all the plain, and all the inhabit-ants of the cities, and that which grew upon the ground."

There was even a massive flood that wiped out every living thing on the earth except for Noah and his family. *Genesis chapters 5-7,* tells of this event.

This is not a God of vengeance. It is a God that loves us but cannot tolerate sin of any kind. God is a God of love and mercy and of light. Sin is in opposition to light, for sin is darkness. Light and darkness cannot be in the same place at the same time. You will either have one or the other.

God gives each of us a choice. Will we live for Him or live with sin in our lives? You will choose either one or the other. Which one you have, will be the one you choose. Choose correctly and you have the love and blessings of God. Choose wrong and you will have the wrath of God. Which one will you choose? The choice is yours.

Joshua 24:15 *"And if it seem evil unto you to serve the LORD, choose you this day whom you will serve; whether the gods which your fathers served that were on the other side of the flood, or the gods of the Amorites, in whose land ye dwell: but as for me and my house, we will serve the LORD."*

Please know that it doesn't matter what you think sin is. What is important is what God calls sin. You can pass laws to justify it, you can even say it isn't so but in the end, God has the last word. If His Holy Word says it is a sin, then it is a sin.

Commit a sin and you will have God to deal with, not man. You are spirit, soul and body. Man can only kill the body. God can destroy all three, the spirit, soul, and body. Make your choice very carefully as to whom you will serve.

Our Choices

Today we are desensitized or brainwashed to wonder if it is all true or is it just something made up. Satan is whispering all of the time, "Did God really say that"? Is all of this really true? How can all of this be? Show me the proof of all this and I'll believe it". Dear friend, I have seen enough proof with my own eyes to know beyond a shadow of a doubt that it is all true.

Hebrews 11:6 *"But without faith it is impossible to please him: for he that comes to God must believe that he is, and that he is a rewarder of them that diligently seek him."*

John 20:29 *"Jesus said unto him, Thomas, because thou hast seen me, thou hast believed: blessed are they that have not seen, and yet have believed."*

If you want to see proof, you must frequent a place where the proof happens. You must look for the proof to be able to see it. Look with your spiritual eyes for the proof. You have spiritual eyes if you are a child of God. We must read our Bible daily. If you are not a child of God, you must be in a place where you can see with your eyes and hear with your ears. Even then, you will probably try to explain the miracle away.

We know that God loves us and is coming back for us. We experience hardships, sickness, and pain like the non-Christian. But God is with us, helping us through all things.

Matthew 5:45 "That ye may be the children of your Father which is in heaven: for He make His sun to rise on the evil and on the good, and send rain on the just and on the unjust." (Here rain means trouble, difficulty or pain)

We may be living as God wants us to but the rain that falls on the sinner sometimes splashes onto us as well. When it splashes onto us, it is to strengthen us and so we will have a witness to His greatness.

Sometimes God moves the hedge of protection back from people or a nation to wake them up. During these times, it is to get them to a place where they will listen. Often when a nation or people see difficult times, they pray to God more. He listens as they pray, obey Him and He comes to their aid.

In the Bible, *Joshua 7:1*, Achan was a man who disobeyed God and the entire nation of Israel suffered for it. In this narrative, Achan was found out and immediately stoned to death along with his entire family.

In our western culture, we may find this harsh. But remember, God and sin cannot abide in the same place. Remember that the wages of sin is death, either physical or spiritual or both. Remember that it is all your choice and no one else's. So be very careful and make your choice even more carefully.

The kind of punishment Achan and his family endured may seem cruel but that was the way it was during the Old Testament times. Achan's family was a part of him and what he did, affected them directly on a grand level.

What we do, greatly affects our family as well. It happens more than one may think. Someone makes a bad choice and they suffer the consequences. What is ignored most of the time is how it affected their family. Most often it causes our families great stress, sadness, hardships, and often financial stresses. There are always negative effects with bad choices and some aren't manifested until years later.

Let's stop for a moment and think about this. Question: Which way seems the cruelest, to have punishment for sin or allow a person to go to hell thinking that they are ok? As for me, I would rather someone tell me that I need to correct something in my life.

But dear friend, we have hope and help. We have the hope and knowledge that God is still on His throne and still in control of everything. We may not see why things appear as they seem or happen as they do. But God has a plan of love and prosperity for each and every one of us. God's plans for us will work out well only if we follow and listen to Him. We must have faith that He will work everything for the good for those who love Him. Then we must be about our Heavenly Father's business telling others of His love.

Romans 8:28 *"And we know that all things work together for good to those who love God, to those who are the called according to* His *purpose."*

Question: If God works everything out for those who love Him and are called according to His purpose, where does that leave the people who choose not to follow Him? How are they making it through this life? How are they dealing with the changing world around us? Where is their hope coming from? Do they even have hope or are they just stumbling through life?

We have hope and faith in God and we know He loves us. We may not understand His approach to our problem but we know He has a plan. Later on, we may see the reason for the way He approached it.

Isaiah 55:9 "For as the heavens are higher than the earth, so are my ways higher than your ways, and my thoughts than your thoughts."

We keep waiting but nothing seems to happen. Oh but my friend, it will all happen one day exactly as the Bible describes. The only question is, will you be ready? Until it does occur, we have God's promise of help in our time of trouble. God is not only our help during tough times, but He is a friend who is always with us. He remains as close as our next breath and our next heartbeat.

According to the Bible, blood sacrifices continued for many years. Question; did you ever wonder which two animal skins God took to cloth Adam and Eve after they sinned?

When Jesus Christ was crucified on the cross, He became the ultimate blood sacrifice for our sins. It wasn't until that ultimate blood sacrifice, that animal sacrifices came to an end for Christians.

John 3:15 "That whosoever believeth in Him should not perish, but have eternal life."

*John 3:16 "For God so loved the world, that He gave His only **begotten** Son, that who-soever believeth in Him should not perish, but have everlasting life."*

John 3:17 "For God sent not His Son into the world to condemn the world; but that the world through Him might be saved."
*John 3:18 "He that believeth on Him is not condemned: but he that believeth not is condemned already, because he hath not believed in the name of the only **begotten** Son of God."*

Jesus being the *only **begotten** son* of God laid down His life to redeem (save) you and me from our sins. He was and is the ultimate sacrifice for our sins. He shed His precious blood on a cross on Calvary to redeem us.   Either we are to be redeemed by this ultimate sacrifice or we are to be sacrificed for our sins.

Question: Does Jesus feel the pain of His crucifixion each time we sin? God help us if He feels the pain of each of our sins. We will have to ask Him when we see Him. I am sure that He is greatly saddened when we sin.

Oh, but when one sinner comes to Jesus Christ asking for forgiveness and repents, all of heaven rejoices. One who was lost and now is found has come home. It is not God's wish that any should be lost but all should be saved and have everlasting life.

Matthew 18:12-14 "How think ye? If a man have an hundred sheep, and one of them be gone astray, doth he not leave the ninety and nine, and goeth into the mountains, and seek that which is gone astray? And if so be that he find it, verily I say unto you, he rejoices more of that sheep, than of the ninety and nine which went not astray. Even so it is not the will of your Father which is in heaven, that one of these little ones should not perish.”

Luke 15:10 “In the same way, I tell you, there is rejoicing in the presence of the angels of God over one sinner who repents”

Matthew 3:2 “And saying, Repent ye: for the kingdom of heaven is at hand.”

What exactly does the word repent mean? It means to ask God for forgiveness for all of our sins. It also means that once you have asked God to forgive you, don't do it again.

John 5:14 “Afterward Jesus finding him in the temple, and said unto him, Behold, you are made whole: sin no more, lest a worse thing come unto thee.”

You have a Friend

Proverbs 22:11 *"He that loves pure-ness of heart, for the grace of his lips the king shall be his friend."*

During my life, I have had many friends or people who I thought were my friends. While some of these friends have been very good ones, others have left me feeling almost friendless. They are your friends just as long as things are going well. But when things begin going wrong, they abandon you at the first sign of difficulty.

Perhaps they are leading you down the wrong path, encouraging you to do things that you shouldn't. There is an old saying that says, "If you lay down with dogs, you get up with flees". Another one says, "Birds of a feather flock together". What does your friend's character say about you to other people?

Many years ago, my son Larry Brentt came home distressed. I asked him, what was the matter? He said that there was a grown man in our neighborhood (we will call him James) that starts shouting and cussing every time he rode by. He said that James wanted to fight him. My son was only sixteen years old at the time.

I told my son to take a ride with me. As we drove past James's house, it was as my son had said. James began heading towards the street shouting, cursing and waving his fist. I stopped to ask what was going on and things only escalated and now James wanted to fight me. A young man in his twenties witnessing the event stepped in front of James. This young man was someone I had befriended years before when he did not have a father figure in his life.

He inquired as I had as to what brought this on. James explained that one of my son's friends had been caught doing something that he should not have. My son knew nothing about what his friend had done but was grouped with that kind of person.

The young man who had stepped in front of James explained that my son was not that kind of a person and that I was of good character. James calmed and he told my son to choose his friends more wisely. I could not have agreed more.

Some people don't have the common sense to come in out of the rain. These friends will lead you in directions that you will wish you had not wandered. Their influence will take you places you should not have gone, keep you longer than you want to stay, and cost you more than you want to spend.

But I have a friend that is far above any friend that I have ever had. This friend sticks closer than a brother. I can talk to this friend at any time day or night. I can tell Him everything without Him turning me away, telling others, or making fun of me.

This friend will never lead me down the wrong path. My friend is always on call and will answer me when I pray. This friend is Jesus. He and His father work together with the Holy Spirit and they guide me moment by moment. The good news is that they will be your friend and guide you too.

There is an old gospel song "What a Friend We Have in Jesus", a Christian hymn originally written

by preacher Joseph M. Scriven as a poem in 1855
to comfort his mother.

What a Friend we have in Jesus,
All our sins and griefs to bear!
What a privilege to carry
Everything to God in prayer!
O what peace we often forfeit,
O what needless pain we bear,
All because we do not carry
Everything to God in prayer.

Have we trials and temptations?
Is there trouble anywhere?
We should never be discouraged,
Take it to the Lord in prayer.
Can we find a friend so faithful
Who will all our sorrows share?
Jesus knows our every weakness,
Take it to the Lord in prayer.

Are we weak and heavy laden,
Cumbered with a load of care?

Precious Savior, still our refuge—
Take it to the Lord in prayer;
Do thy friends despise, forsake thee?
Take it to the Lord in prayer;
In His arms He'll take and shield thee,
Thou wilt find a solace there

At times when I was a child and things didn't go well, I would walk out into an old orange grove. The old two story house that my parents rented was surrounded on three sides by the grove. The tops of the old giant orange trees were high and thick. The tops were so close together that the sunlight never reached the ground. As a result, no weeds or grass grew under the old trees.

There under those orange trees, I would walk and cry to the Lord. It was my time alone with Him where I could tell Him anything and I did. After we had our time together, I would wipe away my tears and walk back home. I would realize on my way back that I felt much better than I did before. Sometimes it just helps to tell a true friend how you are really feeling. God is a true friend and you can talk to Him about anything at any time.

Yes, God is a true friend and much, much more. He is the alpha and omega, the beginning and the end. He is the lifter of my head. He is my healer and my provider. He is my Lord and Savior. He goes before me and fights my battles. He is the very breath that I breathe and my every heartbeat. He is my counselor and guide. He is everything to me and He can be to you as well.

To find God we must diligently seek Him. What exactly does that mean? We must come to the knowledge that He is. We must realize that we need Him. We must pray a prayer of repentance and ask Him to save us and be our Savior. We must read His Holy word daily. This is the only way we will know what His word says and what is in His heart. We must do our very best to live our lives according to His word. We must pray daily according to His word and above all, we must have faith in Him. We must believe in our hearts that he is a rewarder of those who do these things.

Hebrews 11:6 ***"But without faith it is impossible to please Him: for He that cometh to God must believe that He is, and that He is a rewarder of them that diligently seek Him."***

I once had a conversation with my mother. I told her that I was scared of the things the Bible speaks about during the end times, the last days. She told me something that I will never forget. She said, "You must plan for the future but live every day like it is your last". That was undoubtedly one of the most valuable pieces of advice that I had ever received. It was filled with the most common sense ever.

We must plan for the future. I think, "Tomorrow I will mow the grass, God willing". But I must live like today is my last here on Earth. If you have faith in God and know that the Bible is all true, you will live your life differently. You would live your life like you were expecting to meet God face to face at any moment. You would live your life like you expected Jesus to break through the clouds at any moment to call His children home. Are you ready for that moment to happen?

According to the Bible, there is a way to escape the terrible things that will come upon this earth during the end of days. The choice is yours.

Luke 21:36 *"Watch, and pray always, that you may be accounted worthy to escape all these things that shall come to pass, and to stand before the Son of man."*

We know God rewards those who love and obey His word and a punisher to those who do not.

Hebrews 9:27 *"And as it is appointed unto men once to die, but after this the judg-ment:"*

Matthew 10:28 *"And fear not them which kill the body, but are not able to kill the soul: but rather fear him which is able to destroy both soul and body in hell."*

Philippians 2:12 *"Wherefore, my be-loved, as you have always obeyed, not as in my presence only, but now much more in my*

absence, work out your own salvation with fear and trembling."

I hope you remember a few of very important things here.

First: You must have faith that God is. You must be born again. You must ask Jesus to come into your life, forgive you of all that you have done that has caused Him and His Father to be displeased with you, and to be your Lord and Savior. Only then will you be reborn of the spirit. He will show you signs of His presence as long as you are in the right place with Him to see them.

John 3:3 "Jesus answered and said unto him, Verily, verily, I say unto thee, Except a man be born again, he cannot see the kingdom of God."

Second: Pray daily and ask God to help you as you seek Him.

Third: Read God's word daily. You must feed and renew your mind with God's word daily. If not, your soul will starve.

Be very careful about the Bible you read as there is only one path to heaven. A single word changed in the Holy Bible or spoken during a sermon at church can change the meaning completely. This could lead to great eternal consequences.

Song of Solomon 2:15 *"Take us the foxes, the little foxes, that spoil the vines: for our vines* have *tender grapes."*

John 3:16 *"For God so loved the world, that he gave his only begotten Son, that whosoever believeth in him should not perish, but have everlasting life."*

In everyday English, this means that sometimes it is the small and seemingly unimportant changes in the wording that can make the biggest differences.

Be cautious about the church you attend as well. Some churches teach parts of the Bible choosing only the parts they like or agree with. Some churches will not preach or teach about certain subjects in the Bible as they are afraid of losing their tax exempt (501c3) status. Some are afraid of being politically incorrect and offending people. I have heard a pastor say, "If I offend someone within myself, I apologize. But if I offend someone by preaching the whole word of God, you should take it up with God".

Jesus told it like it was and did not worry about being politically correct. God has His rules and guidelines and that is it. No debate or consideration about what is politically correct or incorrect. It is God's way or Satan's way with no debate whatsoever. It is your choice which way you will go when you die, up or down. Choose wisely!

Beware; some churches will mislead you intentionally. In these churches, the pastor is performing nothing more than a job. This pastor was not called of God but was looking for what he thought was an easy occupation. Perhaps that pastor is pushing an agenda that Satan has given him. Oh yes, Satan himself will one day stand up and proclaim to be God. If Satan will do that, he will certainly get his people behind a pulpit to preach. Satan has already infiltrated the church in many places to mislead all of the people that he can.

Revelations 13:11 "And I beheld another beast coming up out of the earth; and he had two horns like a lamb, and he spake as a dragon."

Revelations 13:12 "And he exerciseth all the power of the first beast before him, and causeth the earth and them which dwell therein to worship the first beast, whose deadly wound was healed."

Revelations 13:13 "And he doeth great wonders, so that he maketh fire come down from heaven on the earth in the sight of men,"

Revelations 13:14 "And deceiveth them that dwell on the earth by the means of those miracles which he had power to do in the sight of the beast; saying to them that dwell on the earth, that they should make an image to the beast, which had the wound by a sword, and did live."

True, this type of pastor may very well seem to be a wonderful person living according to what they believe the word of God says. But if they were not called by God to be a pastor, they can only impart part of the truth. Being called of God, they are equipped by God to follow His voice. If they are not following God's voice, they are stumbling around in the dark and taking you with them.

Some of these churches will entice you with things to gain your favor. Some will entice you with dark smoky rooms, loud music, and flashing lights. Question; where will you find that kind of environment outside of that room? Answer: **bars**! There are also many other ways they will entice you. Coffee and donuts in the lobby, etc.....

I have heard it said, "You can change the method but not the message". This may be true for earthly things but not for spiritual things. Sooner or later if you change the method, you will slip into changing the message. At that point, one has stepped out of the will of God.

People called by God will be led by the Holy Spirit. They will be able to share with you a deeper truth connecting the dots so to speak, in the Bible. God and the Holy Spirit impart Holy wisdom that the normal person and the world do not possess.

Some pastors preach only what they are taught in seminaries. Therefore these pastors cannot share the whole, inspired word of God. Go to a church where you can hear the whole word of God. Go to a church where the teachings are not sugar-coated and some parts are omitted. You can follow a map and arrive at your destination but only if you have the whole map. Once you have the correct version of the Bible, read it daily to feed your soul. Each of us needs desperately to feed our soul daily or we will starve it.

Remember, Satan will use every means at his disposal to misdirect people into his trap. He will be very subtle about it, misleading you ever so gradually. He is so gentle about it you won't even realize it is happening to you. That is unless you read your Bible daily and the Holy Spirit opens your eyes to it.

It will be like a spider creeping up on its prey. The prey does not have a clue until the spider springs its trap. At that point, it is too late for the prey. Be wise to the ways of Satan and stay well away from his influence and traps.

According to Wikipedia there is a story of unknown origin:

One evening an old Cherokee told his grandson about a battle that goes on inside of people.

He said, "My son, the battle is between two "wolves" inside us all. One is Evil. It is anger, envy, jealousy, sorrow, regret, greed, arrogance, self-pity, guilt, resentment, inferiority, lies, false pride, superiority, and ego. The other is good. It is joy, peace, love, hope, serenity, humility, kindness, benevolence, empathy, generosity, truth, com-passion, and faith."

The grandson thought about it for a minute and then asked his grandfather: "Which wolf wins?"

The old Cherokee simply replied, "The one you feed."

It is said that the eyes are the windows to the soul. With that being true, feed your soul only the good things. Be careful of what your eyes and ears allow into your soul. Be cautious about what your mouth is allowed to speak.

In today's society, you will undoubtedly hear and see all sorts of things that could send your soul to hell. Avoid the evil things and fill your eyes, ears, mouth, heart, and soul with the things of God. Let your eyes feast on God's word daily. One day very soon, you will be overjoyed that you did. Jesus is going to return soon for His children, are you ready? If your answer is that you are not sure or no, then you can be. You must get ready for His return as it will happen soon.

Please remember this, when a person dies, the world has ended for them. Are you ready for the end of your world? Are you ready to meet Jesus? Wouldn't you like to know that you will be spending eternity in a place much better than this world? If you do not know where you will spend your eternity, there is no time like right now, to get saved and right with God.

Leaving

Proverbs 29:17 "Correct your son, and he shall give you rest; yea, he shall give delight unto your soul."

There is a time for entering, traveling through, and leaving this life. Each person has a set time or number of days to be here upon Earth. Each person's time is not the same for each individual. Not one person knows how long he or she will be upon this Earth. So we must make the most of the time we have here.

Ecclesiastes 3:1 "To everything there is a season, and a time to every purpose under the heaven:"

Ecclesiastes 3:2 "A time to be born, and a time to die; a time to plant, and a time to pluck up that which is planted;"

Ecclesiastes 3:3 "A time to kill, and a time to heal; a time to break down, and a time to build up;"

Ecclesiastes 3:4 "*A time to weep, and a time to laugh; a time to mourn, and a time to dance;*"

Ecclesiastes 3:5 "*A time to cast away stones, and a time to gather stones together; a time to embrace, and a time to refrain from embracing;*"

Ecclesiastes 3:6 "*A time to get, and a time to lose; a time to keep, and a time to cast away;*"

Ecclesiastes 3:7 "*A time to rend* (ip)*, and a time to sew* (plant)*; a time to keep silence, and a time to speak;*"

Ecclesiastes 3:8 "*A time to love, and a time to hate; a time of war, and a time of peace.*"

In the Bible, book of Psalms, we find that David wrote, *Psalms 39:4* "*LORD, remind me how brief my time on earth will be. Remind me that my days are numbered— how fleeting my life is.*"

Psalms 39:5 *"You have made my life no longer than the width of my hand. My entire lifetime is just a moment to you; at best, each of us is but a breath."*

Psalms 39:6 *"We are merely moving shadows, and all our busy rushing ends in nothing. We heap up wealth, not knowing who will spend it."*

Psalms 39:7 *"And so, Lord, where do I put my hope? My only hope is in you."*

Did you know that you can add years to your life? *Exodus 20:12* *"Honour your father and your mother: that your days may be long upon the land which the LORD your God giveth thee."* Following God's command-ments will not only add years to your life but will add joy as well.

Without knowing how many days we will be here on Earth, how will you spend your time? Will we take joy in looking for and acknowledging the good things? Will we try to make things better by doing the right things all of the time? Will we tell others how God has blessed us and share the good news with them?

Psalms 105:1 **"O give thanks unto the LORD; call upon his name: make known his deeds among the people."**

The good news is that God loves you and there is hope for a better day today and for our future. There is hope for a joyous eternity through the forgiving salvation of Jesus Christ. You will never be alone again because God is a friend who will never leave you or forsake you.

When a loved one passes from this life into the next, it is a difficult thing. It is difficult to lose someone that we love. But according to the Bible, we all will pass from this life one day should our Lord linger. According to all of the prophecies being fulfilled and all of the signs of the times that we see every day, we may be raptured up before we die. The rapture could occur before you finish reading this book. However; if we should remain here for a little longer we must endure sorrow and pain.

We sometimes witness our loved ones going to be with the Lord. Losing our loved ones for a short while is not an easy thing to endure. I have often said that funerals are not for those who have passed but for those who remain here.

We feel loss which causes us great pain. But we must temper the feeling of loss and grief with the fact that we know, they are with the Lord if they lived a Christian life. They are where they want to be. They are where they have worked hard to be. Our Christian loved ones had faith and believed in the fact that one day they could rejoice, laugh, and sing with our Lord and Savior.

Our loved ones are in a much better place than we are. Yes, their Earth suits (body) were buried but they are not there. They have gone to be with our Lord.

The problem comes from being here on Earth too long. We have forgotten too many facts about Heaven that we once experienced before our birth. Now for some, there is the human feeling of uncertainty. Rest assured that God is still on His throne and still a God of faithful promises.

He has promised each and every Christian a spectacular and wonderful place with Him for all of eternity. Certainly, we feel the pain of our loss but we cannot allow it to destroy us. We must keep our focus on God and the end goal. Our end goal should be obtaining and maintaining our citizenship in Heaven.

Remember the smiles and laughter of the person who has gone on. What joy and happiness they were feeling in those moments. Now think of how thrilled they must be at their returning home to be with our Lord forever. What excitement and joy they must have felt when they saw Jesus. What happiness and love they must have experienced entering paradise. Now think of the sadness they would feel if they knew what great grief their leaving was causing you.

Why must we continue on without that special loved one? Why must we continue to get out of bed in the morning, fix our faces, brush our teeth, and comb brush our hair? Because we have other very special people in our lives that are counting on us. They deserve our love and support just as much as, the one we are missing. Lose sight of them and their needs, and we have lost much more than you realize.

Yes, it is painful and will remain that way for a very long time. But we need to ask God to give us strength and joy. It is only by His grace that we will mend our heart to where it is tolerable.

Please don't get me wrong. It is ok to grieve for a time but every dark night has a sunrise. There is a better day on its way. We will all pass from this life sooner or later. The only question is, where will each of us spend eternity?

Psalms 147:3 ***"He healeth the broken in heart, and bindeth up their wounds."***

As ***Psalms 147:3*** says, "He heals the broken in heart, and binds up our wounds" but only if we allow Him to. We must lay our problems and grief at Jesus' feet and leave them there. If we pick them back up, it is as though we are saying to Him, "I'll take these because I don't think you can handle my problems". If we don't allow God to handle our problems, He can't. It all comes back to our free will choices. Sometimes handling our own problems is how we got into this mess in the beginning. Let God have His way in your life.

Just as you can add years to your life, you can also take years away. By doing the things that the Bible says not to do, you will subtract years from your life. Have you ever noticed a person who drinks alcoholic beverages and has smoked most of their life? They usually look much older than a person of the same age who has not. Those things are but two that are very hard on your body and will subtract years from your life.

Have you ever heard a person refer to something as theirs? They may have said some-thing like, my car or my house or something similar about some other object. It begins when we are small children that we refer to things as ours. "He took my toy". Stop and think about that for a moment.

Luke 12:18 "And he said, This will I do: I will pull down my barns, and build greater; and there will I bestow all my fruits and my goods."

Luke 12:19 "And I will say to my soul, Soul, you have much goods laid up for many years; take thine ease, eat, drink, and be merry."

Luke 12:20 "But God said unto him, you fool, this night your soul shall be required of thee: then whose shall those things be, which you hast provided?"

Luke 12:21 "So is he that layeth up treasure for himself, and is not rich toward God."

We work our fingers to the bone to gain money so we can gather things and call them ours. Then, when we leave this life our stuff is scattered in every direction. People seem to see just how much of "your stuff", that they can get. Lawyers are made rich by the greed of others as well as their own greed. People seem to be willing to destroy relationships that have taken a lifetime to create over greed. **Fact**: While we are on earth we own nothing. We are only borrowing and managing things while we are here.

Luke 6:35 "But love ye your enemies, and do good, and lend, hoping for nothing again; and your reward shall be great, and ye shall be the children of the Highest: for he is kind unto the unthankful and to the evil".

Mark 8:36 "For what shall it profit a man, if he shall gain the whole world, and lose his own soul?"

Matthew 6:19 "Lay not up for your-selves treasures upon earth, where moth and rust doth corrupt, and where thieves break through and steal:"

So how do we gather things that are of value that we can keep forever? We store up or gather treasures in heaven by living according to God's Holy Inspired word. We share the love of God with everyday people, our friends, our coworkers, and our family and yes, strangers we meet too. We lead others to Christ by living a good example and by telling others what God has done in our lives.

Matthew 6:20 *"But lay up for your-selves treasures in heaven, where neither moth nor rust doth corrupt, and where thieves do not break through nor steal:"*

We lend a helping hand to those truly in need and we should not do so boastfully. If we boast of helping others, we receive our reward here on earth and not in heaven. We do not look for recognition while on earth for our works.

Telling others what God has done for us not only helps others see God's actions but it is a testimony and witness of His love and His great-ness. We overcome Satan by the blood of the Lamb (Jesus Christ) and our testimony to others.

Revelation 12:11 *"And they overcame him* (Satan) *by the blood of the Lamb, and by the word of their testimony; and they loved not their lives unto the death."*

So you may not have lived a perfect life, and who has? There are things in everyone's life that we now wish we would have done differently.

Jesus did not select perfect people to be His disciples. He chose people like you and me.

Jesus chose people who had issues. He chose people who found out there is a better way through Him. Jesus sought people who were real, people who were lost. He sought people who would tell others what He had and what He was doing for them.

Jesus chose people who had a past and could relate to the people they were speaking to. They could explain where they had been in their life, and how Jesus had changed them. People relate better to people who have felt their pain so to speak, people who have walked in their shoes. They can explain how they have a better life now and the wonderful eternal life waiting for them. He chose people who were willing to be used by Him. He chose obedient people like you and me.

Too often people think, God cannot use me with my past. But that is exactly the kind of people God chooses to do His work. They can approach people that others may not be able to. God has work for us to do telling others of His love. Are you ready to work for God? Come on, let's get busy for Him.

Each one of us has a job that God wants us to do. He calls some of us to be preachers. He calls some of us to be song leaders or missionaries. He calls all of us to tell others what He has done for us, to be a witness for Him. What can you do to help others know our Savior? What can you do to encourage them? I am sitting here writing this for you.

God will give you strength to share His word with others. You may be someone who does not enjoy sharing with others. Perhaps you are a little bashful. But if God fills your soul, it will overflow out of your mouth and others will automatically know that you are a child of God. If a person does not realize that God is still in the blessing business, how will they know unless we share our examples of God's love and goodness with them?

Today, some people think that the miracles in the Bible were for the days when Jesus walked the earth. But God's word says that He is the same yesterday, today, and forever. We must share with them that fact and give examples in our lives. Only then will they know, God is still willing to help His children in need.

Hebrews 13:8 "Jesus Christ is the same yesterday, today, and forever."

There is no way that you can hold something in that is so wonderful it makes you smile all over. There is no way that you can contain something so spectacular that it makes your very face light up with joy. So be encouraged and share your joy with others.

I know! Sometimes you don't feel all that joy. But if you begin to share it, you will catch it too. Yes, it is contagious. Start singing a church song and the joy will come. Don't know any church songs? That's ok, begin making up a new song from within your heart and sing that. Songs of praise from the heart bring joy to God.

Psalms 33:3 "Sing to him a new song; play skillfully on the strings, with loud shouts."

When I was in my youth, Pastor Rosa Sikes told my two sisters that they were called to be pastors of God. She told me that I was called to be an evangelist. I was a little jealous of my sisters as I was extremely bashful in those days.

An evangelist is one who usually travels to share the gospel of God, speaks in front of, and meets a lot of new people. Years later, I sit here sharing God's word with everyone who reads this book. I can reach many times more people with God's word, by becoming an author. But no matter what God has called you to do, do it with joy. Do it with all of your heart and you will be greatly rewarded.

Yes, He has something for you to do no matter where you are. Look around you right now. You may or may not like your situation, but there is a reason for it. So, share Jesus Christ with others and it will brighten your day as well as the person you are speaking to.

I hear you! "What if they reject what you are saying?" Don't be discouraged or allow your feelings to be hurt. They are not rejecting you, they are rejecting God. You do your part and let God do His part. You are in sales, God is in management.

It is my firm belief that we have assigned tasks to complete. Remember, God has a plan for each one of us. This belief has been formed by God's word and trial and error, that God will have His way.

First, He has something that He wants to have done and He chose you. He chose you because He has faith in you. He believes you will do a great job performing His task. So He gently and softly whispers to you through the Holy Spirit. But you ignore the whisper.

Next, He allows you to drop that bar of soap on the top of your foot. Go ahead and laugh if you would like to, I did the first time I thought of it. Dropping a bar of hard soap on the top of your barefoot and it feels like dropping a brick on one of your toes. But, you still do not listen to that whispering voice.

Third, God allows something else to slow you down long enough for you to listen. Perhaps it is an injury that takes the wind out of your sails for a bit. But you still do not listen.

Fourth, God withdraws that which He wanted you to do and gives it to another person to do. The other person performs God's task with joy and enthusiasm. Now the other person receives all of the blessings for doing that task. They receive another blessing for being obedient. If what they have done wins another person to God, they receive a soul winning crown as a reward. But there you are, with no reward at all.

Suggestion: be listening to God and His Holy Spirit when He whispers of something that He wants of you. Be eager to say, "Here I am Lord, choose me". It is then that you will receive more than one reward. But by not listening to Him, we receive wrath and judgment that we do not want.

Isaiah 49:1 "Listen, O isles, unto me; and hearken, ye people, from far; The LORD hath called me from the womb; from the bowels of my mother hath he made mention of my name."

Look for only the good things in life. What are the good things in life, you ask? The blessings of God are the only good things worth looking for. It is a certainty that things that are not so good will come your way. But that is when we must lean on God and ask Him to help us through it. Ask Him to give us strength and not to leave us. Lastly, stay away from places and people that are not so good. Remember, what you look for and surround yourselves with, will be what you will have.

Yes, talk is cheap as the old saying goes, so spend all of the words that you have. Tell others what God has been doing to bless your life. Then show others that God's way is the best and only way, by living your life as a good example. The question now is, what has God called you to do for Him?

But until now, you have not been living a good example, you say. Then what on earth are you waiting for? It is a much better life living with God in it. God's blessings are waiting for you. But hurry, as they may not be waiting for you always.

Be Very Careful

Titus 3:8 *"This is a faithful saying, and these things I will that you affirm constantly, that they which have believed in God might be careful to maintain good works. These things are good and profitable unto men."*

During World War II, my dad was in three major battles in Germany. One night during the Battle of the Bulge while in a foxhole, dad made a promise to God. Dad at the time was not a Christian. If dad had been a Christian he would have known that God does not barter. But God was listening, that cold night as bullets flew all around.

God was waiting that night to hear dad pray and call on Him. God had a plan for dad's life just as He has a plan for your life. Dad prayed and promised God that if He would allow dad to return home alive, he would serve Him. Dad served God as a pastor for many years after he returned home.

But be very careful of what you promise God. He is a God of faithful promises and He expects the same from you. If you find yourself in great need of God's help and make Him a promise, do not break that promise no matter what.

Sometimes, it will be a sin problem that placed you in that situation in the first place. You make God a promise, He comes to your aid and then you break your promise to Him. What happens then? You will find that you are in a much worse place than you were to begin with. For when an unclean spirit is cast out of a person, they search for a place of rest but find none. Then the unclean spirit says to its self, "I will return to the place I was before". Keep God in your life and the unclean spirit cannot return.

Luke 11:26 "*Then goeth he* (the unclean spirit), *and taketh* to him *seven other spirits more wicked than himself; and they enter in, and dwell there: and the last state of that man is worse than the first.*"

Sometimes God will allow you to remain in a situation that sin has gotten you into. It is almost as if God is saying, "You knew better but you still did it. Now suffer the consequences of your choices". This is called learning things the hard way. There is an old saying, "Things learned the hard way are best remembered". Meaning, if people get you out of trouble all of the time, you will not struggle. If you struggle, you will remember that struggle and how hard it was for you to get out of that situation. Remembering the hardship, you will refrain from getting in that situation again.

While I was growing up, an honorable man's most binding contract was sealed with a handshake. Today a contract is only as good as the person who signs it and his lawyers. But a promise contract with God should not be entered into unless one is determined to keep it at all cost. Remember, God takes you at your word and He expects you to keep your promises especially to Him.

Deuteronomy 7:9 "*Know therefore that the LORD your God, he is God, the faithful God, which keepeth covenant* (promises) *and mercy with them that love him and keep his commandments to a thousand generations;*"

Once you have asked Jesus to forgive you of your sins, do not turn away from Him. If you turn away, your spiritual condition will be seven times worse than it was before.

Matthew 12:43 "*When the unclean spirit is gone out of a man, he walketh through dry places, seeking rest, and findeth none.*"

Matthew 12:44 "*Then he saith, I will return into my house from whence I came out; and when he is come, he findeth it empty, swept, and garnished.*"

Matthew 12:45 "*Then goeth he, and taketh with himself seven other spirits more wicked than himself, and they enter in and dwell there: and the last state of that man is worse than the first. Even so shall it be also unto this wicked generation.*

2 Peter 2:21 " For it would be better for them not to have known the way of righteousness, than having known it, to turn away from the holy commandment handed on to them."

There is also something spoken of in the Bible called a reprobate mind. God will make sure that you have heard the truth. He will allow you to make the choice to serve Him or serve Satan. He will never force you to live for Him. But there is a point of no return. He will try to gain your love and obedience for only so long. With the continued refusal to serve Him, He may turn a person over to a reprobate mind. So what is a reprobate mind? A reprobate mind is when God allows you to believe a lie to the point that you are damned or lost to sin.

2 Thessalonians 2:11 "And for this cause God shall send them strong delusion, that they should believe a lie:"

2 Thessalonians 2:12 "That they all might be damned who believed not the truth, but had pleasure in unrighteous-ness."

Romans 1:28 " And even as they did not like to retain God in their knowledge, God gave them over to a reprobate mind, to do those things which are not convenient;"

Romans 1:18 "For the wrath of God is revealed from heaven against all ungodly-ness and unrighteousness of men, who hold the truth in unrighteousness;"

Romans 1:19 "Because that which may be known of God is manifest in them; for God hath shewed it unto them."

Romans 1:20 "For the invisible things of him from the creation of the world are clearly seen, being understood by the things that are made, even His eternal power and Godhead; so that they are without excuse:"

Romans 1:21   "Because that, when they knew God, they glorified Him not as God, neither were thankful; but became vain in their imaginations, and their foolish heart was darkened."

Romans 1:22 "Professing themselves to be wise, they became fools,"

Romans 1:23 "And changed the glory of the uncorruptible God into an image made like to corruptible man, and to birds, and four footed beasts, and creeping things."

Romans 1:24   "Wherefore God also gave them up to uncleanness through the lusts of their own hearts, to dishonor their own bodies between themselves:"

Romans 1:25   "Who changed the truth of God into a lie, and worshipped and served the creature more than the Creator, who is blessed forever. Amen."

Romans 1:26   "For this cause God gave them up unto vile affections: for even their women did change the natural use into that which is against nature:"

Romans 1:27 "And likewise also the men, leaving the natural use of the woman, burned in their lust one toward another; men with men working that which is unseemly, and receiving in themselves that recompense of their error which was meet."

Romans 1:28 "And even as they did not like to retain God in their knowledge, God gave them over to a reprobate mind, to do those things which are not convenient;"

Romans 1:29 "Being filled with all unrighteousness, fornication, wickedness, covetousness, maliciousness; full of envy, murder, debate, deceit, malignity; whisperers,"

Romans 1:30 "Backbiters, haters of God, despiteful, proud, boasters, inventors of evil things, disobedient to parents,"

Romans 1:31 *"Without under-standing, covenant breakers, without natural affect-tion, implacable, unmerciful:"*

Romans 1:32 *"Who knowing the judgment of God, that they which commit such things are worthy of death, not only do the same, but have pleasure in them that do them."*

Oh, what a fearful thing that would be, to be turned over to a reprobate mind. My prayer for you is that you listen the first time when God whispers to you and that you are greatly blessed.

Ecclesiastes 8:12 *"Though a sinner do evil an hundred times, and his days be prolong-ed, yet surely I know that it shall be well with them that fear God, which fear before him:"*

Hopefully, you are a child of God already. My hope for you is that you bask in His love every day. Know the joys of God and share them with others.

Mischief

Galatians 5:22-23 *"But the Holy Spirit produces this kind of fruit in our lives: love, joy, peace, patience, kindness, goodness, faithfulness, gentleness, and self-control. There is no law against these things!"*

Someone once asked me if I got into mischief when I was a kid. I have told you the absolute truth thus far, so I must continue. Here I must be like George Washington when he chopped down the cherry tree. I cannot tell a lie, yes and I do not boast of it. I only relate the events of my life to let you know that I am human and have made mistakes. I also relate these events to you as a witness of God's love for us.

My dad worked for the railroad but he was a beekeeper as well and as such had to have a pickup truck. Dad also used this pickup truck to drive to and from work. Dad began working for the

Atlantic Coast Line Railroad when I was two years old. Yes, Dad was a railroad man.

The pickup truck that dad drove was an old 1951 Chevrolet. It had a six, cylinder engine and a three, speed standard transmission. The gear shift was mounted on the steering column, behind the right side of the steering wheel.

It was a fun truck to drive as I remember. You pushed in on the clutch peddle, shifted it into first gear, gave it a little gas, and eased out on the clutch. With enough practice, off you would go. You would drive some thirty feet and shift into second gear. Drive another thirty feet before shifting into third gear. What fun and joy that was.

When dad first bought the old truck, it was painted a sort of grape green color. But with age, it had become rather faded.

There were several areas where rust had started appearing. Dad would take sandpaper and sand the rust away. He took a can of gray primer and sprayed the bare metal where he had just sanded. This left the old truck grape green with large gray areas in various places.

Over time, dad would sand again in another area. This time however he would find that he was out of gray primer. What he did have were a couple of cans of a rusty brown primer. So dad used what he had and sprayed other areas of his truck. This left the truck a grape green with large areas of gray and rusty brown. Oh, did I mention that the truck had a noisy muffler?

Dad sometimes drove the family car to the train depot to work if he was working close to home. As I said earlier, I loved to drive that old truck and shift the gears. I would frequently make up an excuse to take it for a spin and mom would let me. I was all of about sixteen years old at the time.

One day dad drove the family car to work and my cousin Glen and I were out of school. Having nothing better to do, we drove dad's truck to Glen's house across town. There, an idea hit me but we couldn't figure out how to accomplish it.

We drove back to my house and asked mom for her help. I asked her how I could cut a perfect circle out of a piece of paper. Mom took the cover from one of her old Good House Keeping magazines. She folded it in half once and then again. She took a can from her food pantry and placed the can on the folded corner of the paper. Taking a pencil she drew around the can. She cut along the can line that she had drawn and unfolded the paper. **Shazam!** There was a perfect circle cut out in the middle of the paper. I took the paper, thanked mom, and out the door we went. Mom never once asked what the circle was for.

We drove back across town to Aunt Shirley's house, who was Glen's mom. I took a can of silver paint from behind the seat of the truck. We placed the paper with the circle cut out against the outside of the truck. There I spray painted a four, inch polka dot. After several minutes had passed, I took a rag with a little gas on it and rubbed the polka dot just to make sure I could get it back off. Yes, the gas on the rag took it off.

What we did next should have been grounds for a good beating behind the woodshed. We spray painted polka dots all over dad's truck. Remember, it was a grape green with areas of gray and rust colored primer. It looked like a cross between a green milk cow and a clown's suit.

We were so proud of our handy work that we just had to show mom. We drove back to my house and asked mom to come outside. After she stopped laughing, she became very serious. She said in a quiet, serious voice, "When your dad comes home, there was going to be heck to pay".

Shortly after four thirty that day, dad arrived home. He didn't come inside right away so Glen and I followed by mom went out. There stood dad in the yard with his hands on his hips shaking his head. Later we found out that dad was too mad to even say a word.

Dad was very quiet all through supper that night. He didn't say much of anything that night. Dad drove the family car to work for the next few days and was gradually getting in a little better mood. With him starting to accept the fact that his old truck was polka dotted, we didn't see any reason to tell him that we could remove them.

Then came the day that dad drove his truck to work. As he pulled up to work, all of his crew started laughing and teasing him. They said things like, "Boss, don't drive that truck to your beehives. Those bees will think it is a giant sunflower and they will attack it". Dad came home angry again that day.

Over a couple of weeks, dad became a little more accustomed to the polka dots. The old truck still had those polka dots on it when dad finally replaced it with another truck.

To this day I regret decorating dad's truck, sort of. Dad must have had a lot of restraint to tolerate that kind of nonsense. I wonder if I would have had enough forgiveness to turn the other finder (cheek). No pun intended.

Inexperience

Matthew 22:29 "Jesus answered and said unto them, you do error, not knowing the scriptures, nor the power of God."

There is an old saying that says, "What you don't know can't hurt you". I am here to tell you that is not true. What you don't know can kill you.

I have always been good at figuring things out but sometimes that has gotten me into trouble. As an example; when I was about fifteen, my mom and siblings had driven into town. Upon returning home, our family car's engine would not shut off. Mom would turn the ignition key off but the engine would keep running. We found out later that the ignition switch was bad.

The problem for now was how to stop the engine from running. I thought disconnecting the battery cables would do the trick. I looked around for a tool but none were available, so I improvised with something else. Note: Always use the proper tool for the job at hand and don't improvise.

I tried to twist the battery cable connector to loosen it from the battery. I had no idea that car batteries contained an acid that produces an explosive gas. Apparently, there was a spark inside or close to the battery which ignited the gas. Each of the six plastic caps that were screwed in the top of the battery was launched like a rocket.

The plastic caps that did not instantly explode, struck the underside of the hood. They struck it with such force that they shattered into hundreds of pieces. Plastic pieces flew in all directions. Some of the pieces even struck me.

But thank God for prevented that incident from being much worse. My face could have been over the top of that battery as the caps blew off. Battery acid also could have been blown out all over me. But God was there protecting me from what I did not know.

Years later a similar incident occurred. I was working at a car dealership and a customer's car had unexpectedly quit running. I turned the ignition key to restart it, but nothing.

I raised the hood and with my hand checked to see if the battery cables were snug on the battery posts. One cable was loose and there was a spark. The spark was followed by a loud boom and the bottom of the battery blew apart. This allowed all of the battery acid to flow out. But thank God, he protected me yet again.

Looking back I can see now where batteries and I didn't get along very well. On one occasion I had been cleaning the battery terminals on our family car. My wife was saying something as I was finished tightening the cable to the battery. I became distracted as she spoke and took my mind off of what I was doing.

I held the wrench in my left hand as I turned the nut. My wedding ring was in contact with the wrench. The other side of my ring made contact with the battery hold down bolt. This completed the electrical circuit and the gold ring instantly turned a cherry red.

I knew not to pull the ring from my finger or I would pull skin and meat off as well. I dropped the wrench like a hot potato and began spitting on my ring finger. By the time the ring began to cool, my hand was looking like a large cow had slobbered all over it.

I gently twisted the ring and eased it off. There was a blister circling my finger which lingered for several days. But thank God the finger was still there. That was another lesson learned the hard way. Whether from inexperience or just simply taking our mind off of what we are doing for a moment can have difficult consequences.

It is the same with taking our thoughts off of God. Yes, we have to think about what we are doing in the physical but we also have to temper that with being a Christian. We must always keep the things of God in everything that we do. We should not snap back at someone who has just offended us. But if we speak, we should speak as Jesus would, with kindness. If we keep Jesus in the forefront of our thoughts, we will not say the wrong words when we strike our thumb with the hammer. If we keep Jesus in the forefront of our minds, we will reap rewards in Heaven and not punishment here.

1 John 3:6 "Whosoever abides (is) in Him sins not: whosoever sins hath not seen Him, neither known Him."

There is an old saying that, "One good turn deserves another". What in the world does that mean? "One good turn", means something that you have done for someone else that is good. Haven't you noticed? When you do something good, it will always come back to you. But if you do something that is not good, that too will come back to you.

Job 4:8 "Even as I have seen, they that plow iniquity, and sow wickedness, reap the same."

Hosea 10:12 "Sow to yourselves in right-eousness, reap in mercy; break up your fallow ground: for it is time to seek the LORD, till he come and rain righteous-ness upon you."

Hosea 10:13 "You have plowed wicked-ness, you have reaped iniquity; you have eaten the fruit of lies: because you didst trust in your way, in the multitude of your mighty men."

Isaiah 3:10 "Say you to the righteous, that it shall be well with him: for they shall eat the fruit of their doings".

Isaiah 3:11 "Woe unto the wicked! It shall be ill with him: for the reward of his hands shall be given him."

It is way past time for us to do good things all of the time. How do we do that you ask? By keeping our eyes on Jesus! By listening to God and reading God's word. If you hear a whisper coming from inside of you and it speaks of good things, it is from God. If you hear a whisper and it speaks of something that is not good, it is from the devil and will only cause you pain and grief.

How do we know if the whisper is speaking of good or evil? Only by reading your Bible will you know that. You must read your Bible daily. Read in short amounts of time so that what you have read will sink in. I have heard people boasting say,

"I have read the Bible six or seven times. But yet they still live like the devil. That is because they read the Bible without allowing God to help them while they were reading. The devil knows the bible word for word. He just doesn't live by what it says.

It is a proven fact that a person who is asked to memorize a group of ten numbers will only remember the first and perhaps the last two. So at this point, a person will remember only about four numbers. Break the ten digits in half and a person will remember about eight digits. They will remember the first two and the last two of each group. Get the picture? Read your Bible in short time periods, and you will retain more. Allow God to help you and you will remember even more.

Strange Dream

Jeremiah 23:28 *"The prophet that hath a dream, let him tell a dream; and he that hath my word, let him speak my word faithfully. What is the chaff to the wheat? saith the LORD."*

How many times have you wondered about dreams? Why do we dream? Do dreams have meanings? Are they warnings? Are dreams ever instructive or informative?

I have realized over my life that dreams are all of the above. At times they can be any one of the fore mentioned. I believe that dreams on occasion are nothing more than a bored, mind entertaining itself while we sleep. Sometimes it is a mind that has been over stimulated just before sleep.

As I mentioned previously, I was in the Navy and worked on the flight deck, of an aircraft carrier from seven o'clock at night until seven o'clock in the morning.

During flight operations at night, airplanes would be launched and fly off into the darkness. As they were returning to the ship, they would fly a big circle and line up with the back of the ship.

As they came closer to the ship for a landing, you would see the pilot adjust the airplane's approach again and again. First, one wing would dip down slightly and then the other. The pilot kept adjusting and lining up his flight path to the flight deck.

As the airplane came close, you could see small colored lights on the front of one wing constantly changing. This was part of the system that helped the airplane land. The meatball on the ship was the other part of the landing system. There are two horizontal lines of lights that were, end to end. These lights let the pilot know if he was too far to the left, too far to the right, or lined up correctly. There was also a light between these lines (the meatball) to let the pilot know if he was too high, too low, or on the correct descent.

During a carrier landing, you can watch and hear the airplane perform an aerial dance. The wings will dip on one side and then the other while the engines increased power and then decreased power.

One night while aboard the aircraft carrier, I had the strangest dream. I dreamt that I had walked out of the island (super structure) onto the flight deck. The entire deck seemed to be deserted as sunlight bathed the deck. Remember that I always worked at night. The flight deck, being deserted seemed strange as well.

As I began to look around, I looked aft, towards the back of the ship. There in the sky, approaching the ship and coming in for a landing was a large object. With its nose stretched straight out in front of it, it wobbled ever so slightly from left and then right. With ears spread out flat like wings and all four legs hanging beneath it, Dumbo the purple elephant was coming in for a landing. . Yes, you did read that right.

It was about then that I woke up. I have never figured out if there was a meaning behind this dream or just a bored mind entertaining itself. If you can shed some light on this dream, please let me know.

I had more strange dreams while I was aboard the ship. No, there was no alcohol or other mind altering substances allowed aboard our ship.

The next dream was also something strange but could be explained. We had what was called a movie locker aboard ship. While we were in port, our squadron could check out one projector and one movie film per night. We would view it with our squadron but were not allowed to exchange it with another squadron. There was a sailor who took care of and managed the movie projectors and movie films. We were not allowed to pick the movie that we were to watch. The sailor in charge of the movie locker did that for us.

One night we checked out a movie and it was not appropriate for guys aboard a warship. The movie was called something like "Springtime Daisies". We had no choice but to watch it or return it. Our sister squadron received a spy movie which was more suited for a bunch of guys.

We watched our movie almost gaging throughout the entire thing. Then someone had the brilliant idea, "Let's swap movies with our sister squadron". So we swapped movies and began watching the much more appealing movie.

We were down to the last reel when all of a sudden the door to the ready room flew open. In marched the weasel of a guy from the movie locker. He grabbed the movie projector and all of the film, barked something like, "your movie privileges are suspended for three days" and out the door, he went.

Yes, we knew we should not have switched movies with the other squadron, but "Springtime Daisies?" Come on!

Everyone was still furious as we headed back to our berthing (sleeping) compartments. We were still furious as we climbed into our bunks and closed our eyes to go to sleep.

Our bunks were constructed with four chains that were each bolted to the ceiling and the other ends were bolted to the deck. Each chain had three pieces of flat metal bent to look like fishing hooks bolted to it. The bed frame itself looked like a length of pipe bent into a rectangular shape. To the pipe bed frame, thick canvas was sewn with rope lashing. The rope ran through the eyelets by the edge of the canvas, then around the pipe, then through another eyelet, and so on. Then the pipe and canvas bed was placed on the fish hook pieces of metal. There was also a four inch thick mattress placed on top of the canvass.

As the ship gently rolled from side to side, there was a slight and gentle swaying of our bunks. The bunks were three high with the bottom bunk being about six inches above the deck. Each bunk was spaced so there were about twelve inches between your face and the bunk above you. The top bunk was placed so there were about twelve inches between your face and the ceiling.

Sometime during the night, I had a dream. I dreamed that I was in the spy movie and that I was lying on my back on a concrete boat ramp. The hovercraft that was in the movie was coming up the boat ramp (that was a scene from the movie). It was now over me and it began settling down upon my chest. In my dream, I could feel the pressure of the aircushion, and then the weight of the machine on top of me. I was desperately trying to push it up and off of me. I suddenly awoke to my shipmate above me yelling, "Stop, Larry Stop".

In my sleep and in dream, I was pushing the hovercraft off of my chest and preventing it from crushing me. In reality, I had taken hold of my shipmate's pipe bunk frame above me and started bench pressing it upward (shoving it upward). Each time I pushed up, his head bumped against the ceiling, and he was yelling, "Stop, Larry Stop", bump, bump, "Stop, Larry Stop", bump. Yes, we remained friends after I apologized and told him about my dream.

Ecclesiastes 5:3 ***"For a dream cometh through the multitude of business; and a fool's voice* is *known by multitude of words."***

Many years ago I had another dream that may not seem so unusual at first, but wait for the rest of the story.

There was a situation where I could not see myself ever returning to Florida. With every day that passed, I became more resolute in that decision. I thought, "With all of the conflict and hard feelings in Florida waiting for me, I am never going back.

I had been living outside of Florida for a number of years at this point. I had a job and was doing fine, or so I thought. You see, if you are not in the will of God, He will place His plan into action anyway.

I awoke one morning after having this dream and just had to laugh. I dreamt that I was back in Florida and was working a job. That made me laugh out loud. But, God had the last laugh. Within two years I was back in Florida and working for a major electrical utility company from which I retired many years later. Dreams can foretell the future if it is God's will.

Light my fire

Job 1:10 *"Hast not thou made an hedge about him, and about his house, and about all that he hath on every side? Thou hast blessed the work of his hands, and his substance is increased in the land."*

God will place a hedge of protection around His children, their home, and their family and bless the work of their hands.

Years ago while working for a major electrical utility company in the Tampa Bay Area; I worked for a time in the Line Department. I was a Ground man but most of the time I was stepped up to an Equipment operator.

The truck that I drove was an old International truck set up as a corner mount Line Truck. It had a boom with a winch and an auger. An auger is used to drill holes in the ground. In these holes, we placed telephone poles.

As I said, the truck was old. The shift lever coming up through the floor had a rubber dust boot and it had a large hole in it.

One day the driver's door began jarring open while I was driving down the road. I would slam the door closed only to have it jar open a short time later. This went on for a couple of weeks.

One afternoon I attached a pole trailer to the back of the truck and placed a telephone pole on it. I climbed into the old truck and closed the door. With two linemen in a bucket truck following me, we headed for a job site a few miles away. The door remained closed the entire trip to the job. That should have been a warning of things to come.

As we arrived at the job site, I noticed the pole was to be set on the opposite side of the road. I pulled up just past it and started to back the pole trailer into a side road to turn around.

At that very moment, I heard a distinctive sound that sort of sounded like, "POOF". The next thing that I noticed was flames coming up through the hole in the gearshift boot. I turned the engine off and very quickly yanked up on the door handle, but Nothing Happened. The door remained closed tightly. I yanked up on the door handle again while hitting it with my shoulder but Nothing Happened.

Over the truck radio I heard one of the Linemen in the truck behind me yell, "LEO, get out of there, the truck is on fire". I yanked up on the door handle and hit it with my shoulder as hard as I could. I had already decided that if it didn't open this time, I was going to make a door somewhere.

Thank God the door opened on the third try and I jumped out onto the ground some six feet away. The other Lineman ran up with a fire extinguisher and put the fire out.

After the fire, the truck was towed to Tampa for repairs. The fire was started when a power steering hose burst and sprayed fluid on a hot exhaust. The fire had burnt only some wires and the burst hose. Several days later the old truck was back to work. They had also repaired the driver's door latch.

The old truck did fine for about a week. One afternoon I had driven the old truck back to the operation center. I had started to back a pole trailer into its spot when I again hear that distinct loud, POOF. I instantly recognized that sound. I turned the truck off, yanked up on the door handle and the door opened. I jumped out and landed about six feet from the truck. A Lineman again came running with a fire extinguisher and put yet another fire out. After that, they retired the old truck for good.

God has had His hedge of protection around me all of my life. He not only protects me but He has protected my family. If you continue to serve Him, His protection is for you as well.

Years later I had left home headed to work in Tampa. It was a cold winter morning as I left home. I drove about a mile before I smelled it. It was the smell of wood, burning. I thought to myself, "Yep, it sure would be nice to be able to stand around a barrel with wood burning in it on a cold morning like this". I drove a couple of blocks and the smell became much stronger. It grew so strong that I became uneasy and began looking around. It was then that I noticed smoke was coming out of the dash vents in my trucks.

I pulled off of the road at an intersection, jumped out, and raised the hood. Yep, my truck was on fire. I ran into a convenience store, told the man that my truck was on fire, and asked him to call 911. The foreign worker inside the store said, "No"!

It was only then that I remembered my company cell phone was on the seat of my truck. I ran back and called 911. I was able to grab my bible, lunch, and some of my tools out before the flames consumed the truck. The fire department was able to put the fire out, but the truck was a total loss. Once again God was looking out for me as I was unharmed. A little later, God provided me with a newer truck to replace the now crispy one.

The fire had started from oak leaves. They had entered through the fresh air vents below the windshield on the outside of the truck. They then accumulated around a heating element. When I turned the heat on, the oak leaves caught fire.

You know, I didn't think about it until now but with all of the truck fires that I have had, was I being repaid for polka dotting dad's truck? Hum, I wonder......

God Knew Me Before

What a wonderful feeling to know that God knew me before I was born. Wait, that means He knew you before you were born too.

Jeremiah 1:5 ***"Before I formed thee in the belly I knew thee; and before you camest forth out of the womb I sanctified thee,*** **and I ordained thee a prophet unto the nations."**

So God knew you and He knew me before we were born. He had a plan for my life and He has a plan for your life as well. Can't you picture it in your mind's eye? God is the creator of not only everything but the creator of every soul as well.

God created each human being with different attributes, different abilities, for different tasks. He knew the tasks that would need to be performed and what skills would be needed for each task. No one can perform your tasks as well as you.

So, God in His infinite wisdom created you for something very special. It is up to you to say, "Yes Lord, I will do it". If however, you choose not to do it, He will give the task to someone else to do. Then they will receive the blessing and you will not. Are you ready to say, "Yes Lord"?

After we are born, we still retain the memories of our life in heaven. We remember who God is and who Jesus Christ is. We knew them both as we spent many hours with them. We had memories of how beautiful heaven is, full of peace, joy, and love.

Years ago when my grandson Dustin was a small boy, he saw Jesus. We had been taking him to church. At the time I was a greeter and the head usher. So I put Dustin to work in church for God. I would have him stand beside me just inside the church door and greet people as they came in. I instructed him to say "Nice to see you this morning", stick his little hand out to shake hands. I told him to squeeze the men's hand as he shook it but be gentle with the ladies. Dustin was all of about five at the time.

One Sunday while the pastor was delivering the message, Dustin leaned over to His grandmother and said, "There's Jesus". To which my wife replied, "Where honey"? Dustin said, "Standing over there in the corner, don't you see him"? My wife and I both looked but saw only the pastor on the platform still delivering the Sunday message. My wife asked Dustin what Jesus was doing and Dustin replied, "Just standing there, watching". I am convinced that he saw what he claimed to have seen as little children were always very special to Jesus.

Don't forget that little children still partially remember things they were familiar with in Heaven. They have not yet been fully desensitized here on Earth. Once fully desensitized, their memory of Heaven, knowing Jesus and what it was like there, will all but be erased. Sad isn't it? The most wonderful things a person could ever know, all replaced in a few short years by the hustle of life on earth.

Dustin went to be with the Lord in 2020 and has regained the love and peace he once knew.

Dustin was a man of God who served his community as an EMT Firefighter. We will be with Dustin again one day and our love will still be very strong for him. He is still a very precious person in our hearts.

Luke 18:16 "But Jesus called them unto him, and said, Suffer little children to come unto me, and forbid them not: for of such is the kingdom of God."

Jesus loves little children because of their tender hearts and trusting spirits. But something happens to us that is not good or expected before leaving heaven. We begin to become desensitized. From birth, we hear people say words that they should not say, like curse words. We begin to hear people tell things that we know are not true. We see things on television that should not be shown. You may be watching a family TV show and then the commercial comes on. Yes, an awful lot of damage can be done in a few minutes of watching commercials of upcoming shows. It gets worse, much worse. Then we are sent to school and exposed to the school system's teaching. They will require you to study gods of other countries but you can't mention Jesus Christ or the God America was founded upon.

Before long a child is beginning to wonder if the Bible isn't just another book. It is at this early age that the devil tries to enter the human mind. Attack them at an early age before they can retain the heavenly things permanently. But thank God, Dustin held on to his Christian spirit.

It was Dustin's little brother Nickolas that confirmed to our family, that little children retain their memory of heaven.

My wife and I were in the living room of our home. We had a Christian program on the television. As Nickolas walked out of the hallway and into the living room, the pastor on the TV said the name of Jesus. Nickolas stopped as though he had walked into a glass door. He jerked his head towards the TV, stared, and listened intently. He stood there without moving a muscle for a long time before he joined his brother on the couch. We never asked Nickolas what he was thinking as he listened that day but now I wish we had.

After our daughter had Nickolas, she had a miscarriage and lost the baby. Years later our daughter became pregnant again. This time her third son named Seth was born. They had never told Seth anything about the miscarriage.

Early one morning Seth came downstairs and asked his mother if she knew he had a sister. He informed her that he had met her during the night. He told his mother that she had long brown hair and was very pretty. He told his mother that she was happy to see him but just would not stop hugging him. Seth was about five years old at the time that he told his mother about this encounter with his sister. Stephanie thought, "Well it's time to tell him about the miscarriage". This happened many years ago and our daughter did not have any other children.

Seth remembered more than he was saying when he was much smaller. No one told him at age three what to look for to decide if a building was a church or not. At the time, their family was not attending church. As his mother would drive through the town they live in, they would pass by churches. Each time they passed a church Seth would say from the backseat, "There's a church". How could he have known? What drew him towards churches?

At age five Seth was attending church with our whole family. During a service, Seth told his mother, "I am crying, I am happy but I am crying". His mother softly explained that it was the Holy Spirit that he was feeling and that it was good.

The Holy Spirit is the comforter of our soul. The Holy Spirit also lets us know when things are right or not right.

Some people may doubt these accounts. They would contribute these accounts to a child's imagination. But please remember that we adults have been desensitized to this world to a great degree. It is only when we seek God and look at things through a child's eyes that we will see the true picture of things. May I suggest that children have a more realistic view of spiritual things than we adults? It is the adults who have lost the most truth and not children.

John 14:16 *"And I will pray the Father, and he shall give you another Comforter, that he may abide with you forever;"*

John 14:26 *"But the Comforter, which is the Holy Ghost, whom the Father will send in my name, he shall teach you all things, and bring all things to your remembrance, whatsoever I have said unto you."*

When you are seeking a home church, you must test the spirit. Attend the church of your choosing a few times. If you don't feel God's Holy Spirit, find another church. If they are teaching and preaching out of an altered version of the Bible, find another church. Remember John 3:16!

John 3:16 *"For God so loved the world, that he gave his only* **begotten** *Son, that whosoever believeth in him should not perish, but have everlasting life."*

If the word **begotten** is not in that verse in the Bible that they are teaching and preaching from, the devine bloodline of God has been removed.

We had such great hopes when we left heaven headed to our mother's womb. But then we became desensitized to the world and lost the best part of ourselves. We must work hard to regain as much of what we lost as possible.

Sometimes we spend our entire lives here on Earth seeking but never fully finding what we have lost. To gain part of that back, we must become a child of God once again. To find joy once again we must give our lives to God where it is safe. We must look to Him for our strength, our help, our peace, and our salvation. It is only by living for Him that we regain our joy and enter heaven for a much greater reward than what we can find here. If you want love and peace, joy, and help in the times of trouble, find and live for God.

Final question; Are you aiding the world in desensitizing your children? Are you placing Earth blinders on your child? Or are you helping them retain the memories of Heaven? If you are helping them retain the memories of Heaven, then you are setting a good example for them. You are also taking them to a good church.

If you are not helping your child retain the memories of heaven, hold onto your hat and stand by for rough weather. God is not pleased with you. You will be held accountable before God for not taking your children to His house. You will also be held accountable before God for not setting a good example before them.

Proverbs 17:13 "Whosoever rewards evil for good, evil shall not depart from his house."

Proverbs 22:6 "Train up a child in the way he should go: and when he is old, he will not depart from it."

Deuteronomy 4:9 "Only take heed to thyself, and keep thy soul diligently, lest thou forget the things which thine eyes have seen, and lest they depart from thy heart all the days of thy life: but teach them thy sons, and thy sons' sons;"

Proverbs 3:7 "Be not wise in thine own eyes: fear the LORD, and depart from evil."

Tyler's Prayer

About eight years before the writing of this, I was in the middle of trimming an oak tree in our front yard. Once the small oak branches were clipped and had fallen to the ground, my wife would pick them and deposit them on a trailer. We were almost finished when she told me she wanted to look to make sure I had leveled the underside of the tree. Sandra walked to the neighbor's driveway, turned around, surveyed the tree, and smiled. I thought, "I am home free, and doing well with the tree.

As Sandra walked back to our yard, she walked right past me and headed to the house. I thought that was odd but did not question it. A few minutes later I was summoned to the house and was told to rush her to the hospital. It seems that on her way back from the neighbor's driveway, she had started experiencing tightness in her chest that kept getting worse.

I rushed her to the hospital about three miles away. They rushed her in and within a very short time confirmed that she had experienced a heart attack. A cardiologist was called in and an operation was scheduled.

A triple heart bypass was performed and she was taken to the cardiac intensive care unit. She remained heavily sedated for the next four days which I was told was unusual. Apparently, the anesthesia they had given her during the operation, did not agree with her.

The first evening came after the operation and I was still by my wife's side. The nurse informed me that I could not stay overnight as it was against hospital policy. So I said to my wife, "I'll see you in the morning" and went home. My wife was still heavily sedated and knew absolutely nothing, but I talked to her as though she was fully awake.

It wasn't until the next morning when I returned to the hospital that I got the news. About twenty minutes after I left the night before, her heart went into atrial fibrillation. That is just a fancy term meaning that the upper chambers of the heart began beating way too fast. It can cause blood clots and even death. They were able to get her heart back to normal.

The second night, I left the hospital later than the night before and the same thing occurred again. About twenty minutes after I had left, her heart went into atrial fibrillation again. The third night, I decided to handle my leaving differently. She was still not awake from the sedation and did not know of anything going on around her, or so we thought. The third night I said my good night to her as usual and headed towards the door. I pushed the door open and let it close. I stood quietly inside her room for thirty minutes and nothing happened out of the ordinary. So I quietly opened the door, eased out, and headed home.

I had not gone far when the hospital called me and asked me to return. It seemed that shortly after I had left, the atrial fibrillation happened again. Somehow she knew when I had actually left. The love we have for one another is a wonderful thing. It is also strange to know that it is sometimes linked to our very health.

With this happening within twenty minutes after I left each night, it changed my situation. The nurse told me that if I wanted to stay overnight and I promised to remain in the room during shift changes, she would allow it.

So I remained in the room doing as I had the days before. I would softly pray and read the Bible while sitting beside her bed. The presence of God was very strong in that room. On day two I began feeling a very strong presence over in the corner. By day four, I knew there was something in that corner but I could not see it. It was very tall, very peaceful, loving, and kind, but very powerful. The feeling of that presence became so strong that I took out my cell phone and took a picture. It wasn't until weeks later while showing my sister that she pointed out seeing a wing of an angle in the picture.

On day five, she was awake and moved to a normal room. I was there and walked with her and the nurse as they moved her. As she was entering her new hospital room, the cardiac nurse told the nurse on that floor, "She is only doing as well as she is because he is here (meaning me). He is allowed to stay overnight"! It was because I was praying and reading the word of God out loud that was allowing her to do better.

We remained in the hospital for another week. The anesthesia given to her during the operation had done something to her taste buds. Everything she tasted seemed horrible. She could not eat or drink anything. Even water had a horrible taste to her. By day six, I was very worried.

It was at the beginning of day seven that she said, "I would like sliced peaches from Golden Corral. So several times a day I would travel a half mile to get her peaches. I brought back every kind of ice cream, bottled water of various brands, and other things, but she could only nibble on those peaches. Crushed ice was all she could tolerate and those peaches.

Then came the day when she was to come home. She went straight to bed wearing an oxygen tube. She lay in bed for a couple of days unable to get up even for a moment without help.

Then one night, at age three, Tyler decided to go in and check on Grand mommy. Tyler is our son Larry Brentt's youngest son. No one had noticed that he wasn't in the living room with the rest of us.

He eased down the hall and into Grand mommy's room and up beside her bed. He asked her very softly, "Are you sick Grand mommy"? She stretched out one arm and placed it around the shoulders of the dark haired, brown eyed little Tyler. It was then that the top of her incision was reviled to him. Little Tyler asked her, "What happened, did a dinosaur bite you"? My wife smiled and said that she had an operation. To which little Tyler replied, "Do you want me to pray for you"? She told him, "Yes" and Tyler began to pray. He said, "Dear God, please heal my Grand mommy", Amen.

Remember, prayers don't have to be, long with many words. You don't always need to pray for hours for God to hear you. Prayers from a pure heart mean more to God than the number of words in a prayer.

Each night after that, Tyler would enter her room by himself and pray for his Grand mommy. Each night he would add a few more words to his prayer. One night after he finished praying for my wife, he said, "Now I am going to pray for Maw-maw", which is his grandmother on his mother side of the family.

Then, one night while Tyler's mother was cooking supper, Sandra walked into the kitchen and said, "Are ya'll trying to starve me"? Praise God who had heard the prayers of a precious little prayer warrior and had answered those prayers.

It had been a total of about two and a half months from the time of my wife's heart attack to her regaining her strength. She had lost a total of thirty pounds from not being able to eat anything but peaches.

Sometimes we pray and receive an instant answer to our prayers. Other times we pray and the answer comes later. We must remember that it is not always in our timing that we receive the answer but it is in God's timing. We must keep our faith and trust in Him.

~ 136 ~

It is when we humble ourselves as little children that we reach God's heart. It is then that He has the most compassion for our needs and requests. It is my prayer that Tyler never loses his humble and tender heart and that he remains a man of God all of his life. Tyler has a very special work that God wants him to do.

Dark Flight Deck

James 4:10 "Humble yourselves in the sight of the Lord, and he shall lift you up."

We cannot do anything ourselves. It is only with God's help that we breathe and our hearts beat. It is by remaining humble, giving Him all of the glory, our praise, and worship will we prosper.

Galatians 6:9 "And let us not be weary in well doing: for in due season we shall reap, if we faint not."

We should bless others every time we have a chance. Look for opportunities to bless others and we will also bless ourselves.

James 4:17 "Therefore to him that knoweth to do good, and doeth it not, to him it is sin."

You will note that all of the good promises of God contained in the Bible are for the children of

God. Yes, you read that correctly. If you are not a child of God, you have only one promise of God.

1Peter 3:12 *"For the eyes of the Lord are over the righteous, and his ears are open unto their prayers: but the face of the Lord is against them that do evil."*

You have the promise that Jesus Christ is listening for a prayer of repentance. He is listening for you to ask for forgiveness of all of your sins. He is also listening for you to ask Him to be your Lord and Savior. Once we have prayed that prayer and meant it with our whole heart, we are saved and a child of the most high God.

1 John 1:9 *If we confess our sins, he is faithful and just to forgive us our sins, and to cleanse us from all unrighteousness.*

1 Timothy 2:5 *"For there is one God, and one mediator between God and men, the man Christ Jesus;"*

I stated earlier, that God is a friend who will never leave us provided we are one of His children.

In 1967 I joined the United States Navy. I was fortunate enough to be assigned to a squadron after boot camp. Our squadron was first assigned to the USS Essex. Later, I would be assigned to the USS Wasp, both out of Quonset Point, Rode Island.

During the two years that I had sea duty, we went to sea many times. Some of the cruises were short and several were longer, lasting months. During all of those cruises, my job with this anti-submarine squadron was on the flight deck.

I worked from seven o'clock at night to seven o'clock in the morning. We worked seven days a week for the entire time we were at sea. If we pulled into a port, we worked twenty four hours on duty and forty eight off.

We crossed the Atlantic Ocean visiting seven different countries, crossed the Arctic Circle tracking a Russian submarine, recovered the Apollo 7 astronauts, and their space capsule and even traveled through the Bermuda Triangle several times. God went with me wherever we went.

I did a google search once and asked how dangerous it was to work on the flight deck of an aircraft carrier. Google stated that a flight deck was the most dangerous five acres on planet Earth.

The flight deck of an aircraft carrier is an almost maddening flurry of activity. There were aircraft taking off, aircraft landing, aircraft practicing approaches, aircraft carrier landing qualifications, and other activities. All of this took place on five acres. It is like a carefully directed ballet but with airplanes and people in very close proximity to one another.

The noise on a flight deck is almost deafening. We wore noise suppressing ear muffs but it was so noisy you still could not hear yourself think. Not only did we have aircraft with propellers but we had jets as well.

During the day you could see the propellers spinning while the engines were running. At night, it was different. You only knew where they were supposed to be. There was no visual aid to confirm a spinning propeller was present.

After dark, all of the white lights that can be seen on the outside of a navy ship are turned off. The only lights that are visible are red in color. Red lights can only be seen a short distance away from a ship at night. White lights can be seen for many miles.

Normally, the night skies are filled with more stars than you could possibly count. With a bright moon and the stars, you can make out the outline of the navy destroyers running a few miles away off to our sides.

There was one night however that opened my eyes. On one very rare night, there were no flights. I ventured out onto the flight deck in the wee hours of the morning. I was utterly amazed at the contrast, of a normal work shift and this night.

On this particular night, the moon and stars were not to be seen. As I stepped out onto the flight deck and closed the hatch behind me, darkness poured over me. I not only, could not see the moon and stars but I could not see any other ships. It was so dark that I could not see our own flight deck or the edge of it.

I could feel the constant wind as the huge ship plowed through the sea in utter darkness. There was also the pressure of my feet against the flight deck surface.

The darkness was so intense that it wrapped around me like a plastic bag. Heavy, thick darkness pressed ever tighter and tighter against my entire body. It seemed to fill my nostrils and air passages. It felt almost as though the darkness was thick enough to stop me from breathing.

I could feel the gentle vibration of the ship against the bottom of my feet. Normally after a few days aboard ship, this sensation was no longer noticed. I became aware of trying to breathe as the darkness seemed to grow thicker.

Standing there alone, I realized how small and insignificant I really was. I was not even a tiny speck out here. I thought, "If someone fell overboard on a night like this, they would never be found".

Although there were some three thousand sailors below my feet, I felt totally abandoned. It was then, just before panic flooded in that I remembered, I am never alone. God is always with me. He will never leave me or forsake me. The Bible assures me that I have a friend in Jesus!

I opened my mouth and prayed, Heavenly Father I thank you that you are mindful of me. I thank you for your love and grace. I thank you that you let me see just how insignificant I am in the scheme of things. I thank you for keeping me safe and being there with and for me. Amen

Psalms 8:3 When I consider thy heavens, the work of thy fingers, the moon and the stars, which you hast ordained;

Psalms 8:4 What is man, that you art mindful of him? and the son of man, that you visit him?

I remained fairly close to the island or superstructure as it is called. As I turned around, I could barely see the dim red light leading me back inside. I was thankful for that experience and what God had shown me. I thank God for reminding me that He is always with me no matter where I may be and that He will never leave me. His guiding hand will always lead me safely back home. This is the first time that I have ever shared that experience.

At times you may feel down and out. You may feel insignificant and out of place. But when you are at your lowest, remember God loves you and wants only the very best for you.

Remember to ask Him to forgive you of all of the things you have done wrong. Ask Him to be your Lord and Savior and mean it with all of your heart.

Listen to and follow Him so that your days may be many upon the Earth. He will lead you during thick and thin when it feels like everyone else has given up on you. Live your life for Him, not wavering but giving Him the praise and glory for everything. Know that He has your best interest in mind. Tell others what He has done in your life and live a Godly example. You will most certainly be rewarded on Earth and in the life that is surely to come. Know that I am praying for everyone who reads these, God's words. No matter where your darkest hour finds you, remember God is right there with you. Be greatly blessed and know that

God loves you and is working things out for you even as you read this.

God Wants to Prosper You

Yes God wants to prosper you. He wants to be your friend, provider, protector, and healer. Jesus Christ is my Lord, God and savior and He is my rock in the time of trouble. God is my strength and refuge when things go wrong. He is my source of everything good. When I don't know what to do or need help, I can always call on Him at any time. When I am lost for words or have lost my direction, and don't know where to turn, He will always be there.

When I have a problem I can lay it at Jesus' feet for Him to take care of. Once I lay something at Jesus' feet, I try not to worry about it anymore. For if I worry about it, it is as though I am doubting His ability to take care of it. I must hold onto my faith and belief that He is working in my behalf.

Sometimes God does not respond the way that I prayed. I may ask God to fix something, and it seems as though He doesn't. It is at that moment that I realize He is working on something else for me. He has a plan I just don't know what it is at the moment. But someday I will see His plan come together.

Romans 8:28 " And we know that all things work together for good to those who love God, to those who are the called according t His purpose."

Psalms 1:3 "And he shall be like a tree planted by the rivers of water, that bring forth his fruit in his season; his leaf also shall not wither; and whatsoever he doeth shall prosper."

Genesis 18:19 "For I know him, that he will command his children and his household after him, and they shall keep the way of the LORD, to do justice and judgment; that the LORD may bring upon Abraham that which he hath spoken of him."

Know that the good promises of God are for His children. If you are not a child o God, the good promises contained in the Bible are not for you. For non-Christians, there are promises of wrath and judgement. I know that if you are not a child of God, right now you want to be. You want the good promises, a wonderful life here, and in the next life that is sure to come.

3 John 1:2 *"Beloved, I wish above all things that thou mayest prosper and be in health, even as thy soul prospereth."*

Perhaps you are saying, "But I have always been a good person. I go to and belong to a church". To which I reply, "I go to fast food places to eat, but that doesn't make me a hamburger". We must have a personal relationship with our Lord and Savior Jesus Christ.

There is a quick and easy way that you can have the good promises of God and live in His blessings. You can become a child of God. It is so simple to become a child of God. How about it, are you ready? Wonderful, repeat after me and you must mean it with all of your heart.

Heavenly Father, God of Abraham, Isaac, and Jacob, until now I have not lived my life for you. I know that Jesus Christ was the sacrifice for my sins. I know that Jesus Christ is the son of the living God. I know that He was slain for my sins and that He arose three days later. I ask you to forgive me of all sin and wrong doing in my life. Cover me in the sacrificial blood of Jesus Christ. Jesus, be my lord and savior. I will read your Holy word and live my life according to it. In Jesus' holy name I pray. Amen

What a wonderful day this is. It is one of the best days of your life. Now you can claim the good promises of God. Right now, all of the angels in heaven are shouting for joy and saying words of encouragement for you. Can't you hear them? They are saying, "Welcome home, and Welcome to where you belong". Now you are a joint heir with Jesus Christ in the family of God.

Don't forget to find a good Bible that has the word 'begotten' in John 3:16. Read your Bible every day to feed your soul. If you don't, your soul will starve. Find a good church and attend. Do not look at the other people in church with you. But keep your focus on worshiping God. Remember, if you do see someone in Church that you know is not right with God, perhaps Church is exactly where they need to be. Hopefully, some of it will rub off onto them. Pray for them that the Holy Spirit will draw them to God.

Jeramiah 31:3 *"The LORD hath ap-peared of old unto me, saying, Yea, I have loved thee with an everlasting love: therefore with loving kindness have I drawn thee."*

Meet the Author

Born in the fall of 1949 in central Florida and have lived here most of my life. My spiritual roots grew in the Ruskin Tabernacle which was an Apostolic Church.

My family's Christian roots began at the Ruskin Tabernacle under the ministry of Pastor Rosa Sikes. God surely filled this little church with His presence and miracles.

While in high school, I attended high school by day and a bible school in Lakeland, Florida by night.

In 1967 I joined the US Navy and served with an antisubmarine squadron aboard two aircraft carriers, the USS Essex and the USS Wasp. I served for two years aboard these aircraft carriers while on sea duty. I attended a military school in Tennessee for advanced training. The remainder of my naval service was spent working on jet engines and served as flight crew with a training squadron in Maryland.

During my life, I have seen many wonderful miracles. These were divine miracles from God and there was no doubt about it. These events occurred within my family. I knew the situation before the miracle and after as well. I knew without a doubt that these were miracles from God.

During the summer of 2019, God instructed me to write a book for my children and grandchildren. The book was to enlighten my family to the things of God that I had witnessed within my own family. I also wanted to share with them the blessings, promises, protection, and love of God that I have enjoyed during my lifetime. I wanted to present these in a practical, everyday way so they could relate to them in their daily lives. So I began and continue to write.

I include God's word in my writings along with true life examples. Perhaps some of the examples are humorous but all are intended to give God all of the glory. It is only by His love and grace that I am still here to share with my family, and you, my friends.

It is with sincere gratitude that I would like to thank you for reading this book. I truly hope this book has been a blessing to you in some small way. If you have enjoyed this book, please consider being kind enough to leave a review on Amazon.

You may search Google.com or go to **amazon.com/author/larryoneal** to find this book and the other books that I have written.

Until we meet in Heaven,
May God richly bless you is my prayer.

All verses are taken from various versions of the King James Version of the Holy Bible.

Made in the USA
Columbia, SC
22 September 2022